Fit and Flourish:

Discover How God Created You
to Make a Difference

All because of grace

Tim Roehl

I Cor 15:10

Tim Roehl

Dedicated to
Our Grandsons
Ian and Xavier...
and our grandchildren yet to come...

May our legacy of following Jesus
empower you to trust the Lord
bigger and sooner
in your generation
than we did in ours.

Fit and Flourish:
Discover How God Created You to Make a Difference

For more information and resources:
Website: www.timroehl.net
Email: TimRoehl@usfamily.net
Facebook: timroehl
Twitter: @timroehl

Table of Contents

Endorsements

"Tim has devoted his life to helping others to "fit & flourish." The coaching provided in this book is relevant whether someone is initially exploring ministry or seeking greater clarity after years of ministry. His insights are infused with encouragement that keep you motivated to seek God's best for you!"
--Dr. Wayne Schmidt, General Superintendent, The Wesleyan Church

"If you're someone considering your calling-- whether for a season or a lifetime--and want to spend some time reflecting on how God has wired you and prepared you, *Fit and Flourish* is worth the read."
--Dr. Bob Logan, Author, Trainer, World-renown expert on leadership, www.loganleadership.com

"Tim's writing style is right up my alley. I'm sure I'm not alone when I say I want books for those I coach or oversee that are simple tools, yet with real depth. This is such a book. His use of the coaching questions contained in each chapter are timely and help you interact with the challenge of each chapter. I believe this book is going to become a hallmark tool for discovering the call of God in believer's lives and then putting in place a healthy plan to get to that calling."
--Dr. Ray Van Gilst, District Superintendent for the Central Pacific District, C&MA.

"Tim Roehl has done it again! With the heart of a shepherd, the eye of an artist and the toolbox of a craftsman, Tim's newest book, *Fit and Flourish*, will help you find your niche and grow in effectiveness. But be warned, his practical, potent and provocative insights will not let you off the hook with "five simple steps" or "imagine your way to greatness." No, this is high octane, no nonsense counsel from one of the best in the world at helping leaders do just as the title says, "fit and flourish." If you're wondering about your next step, or wanting to grow as a person and as a leader you will do well to pick up a copy today. You will be glad you did, because you will never be the same."
--Tom Clegg, Clegg Consulting Group, Des Moines, IA

"*Fit and Flourish* is a guide to understanding who you are and your best contribution. When we function in the ways God uniquely created us, we experience meaningful purpose and make a powerful impact. Tim Roehl provides a holistic approach to finding your fit, so you can flourish!"
--Dr. Keith E. Webb, Author, *The COACH Model for Christian Leaders,* President of Creative Results Management

"*Fit and Flourish* is an interactive journey in search of the best "me" or the best "you." While telling some of his story, Tim helps us discover our stories. Weaving Scripture, his own experiences, soul-grabbing illustrations and word pictures, Tim helps us become, arrive and thrive. *Fit and Flourish* helped me revisit my spiritual roots and the simplicity of walking with Jesus. Tim, through *Fit and Flourish*, coaches us toward better self-awareness, new levels of spiritual health, clarity and confidence as we exercise our gifts and graces. Read...slowly, purposefully! Allow the coaching questions to guide your journey."
--Rev. Les Cool, Pastor and Head of The Kingdom Extension Community, Evangelical Congregational Church

"I have had the distinct pleasure of serving with Dr. Tim Roehl in multiple roles since 2002. His latest book reflects a careful weaving of personal anecdotes, like the Roehl Family Motto, journal entries and prayers with a very clear and challenging call for us to be all that God desires for us to be. Using a series of "Looks," Tim guides the reader through a penetrating look at his/her own life with God. These "looks" are enhanced greatly by Tim's careful and accurate exegesis of Scriptures such as Jeremiah 6:16. Each section is further developed by carefully crafted exercises titled, *Coach Yourself Forward,* in which readers are assisted in evaluating themselves. These exercises reflect well Tim's expertise in coaching and using open-ended questions. Dr. Roehl winsomely invites readers to examine their own spiritual journey to make sure they are where God has fitted them so they can experience the Holy Spirit empowering them to flourish. In my current role with missions, I am especially pleased that Tim has the section titled, "Look Out," where he presents the opportunities awaiting believers today for what

matters most to God. Because of the many exercises, anecdotes, stories and references, I believe you will find this book to be a constant companion on your journey to be all God desires you to be. Enjoy, practice and soon you will be saying, *"Whee!"*
--Rev. William (Bill) Vermilion, PhD, member of Theological Education Team, One Mission Society, Inc., former Seminary Professor and Academic Dean, past General and Conference Superintendent, The Evangelical Church

"This is Tim's best book yet. The reason, of course, is because the subject matter is in the area where he fits and flourishes in his own life. Tim is among the world's best ministry coaches and assessors. This book will be a great tool to help multiply his work, virtually allowing him to be in thousands of places at the same time."
--Rev. Neil A. Stevens, church planter and coach (trained and mentored by Tim)

"Tim's latest book, written from his own personal style as a master coach, makes it both rich in wisdom, yet reader friendly. The solid messages and recommendations for Kingdom leaders are creatively clear. Likewise, Tim's challenge for ministers to be Kingdom leaders instead of their own personal 'empire builders' is a relevant and needed message for today. Tim's essential qualities for spiritual pioneers are relevant and insightful. As ministers, we want what Tim is prescribing. I recommend Tim's book to men and women of God, who are seeking to be authentic and Christ-like ministers of the Gospel. I believe this book will assist readers in knowing how to 'fit and flourish' in their respective roles in the Kingdom."
-- Dr. Carolyn Knight, Church Multiplication Facilitator at One Mission Society, author of *In Search of Persons of Peace: Inspirational Stories of How Ordinary People Inspire Multitudes for Christ*

"In a world that idolizes the successful, Tim invites us into something better--to be God's original master piece. In "Fit and Flourish," Tim invites followers of Jesus to go on a journey where they can discover and discern who God created them to be and to boldly live that out where God has placed them."
—Greg Langman, New Venture Development Director, C&MA Canada

"Our calling comes from God, but God brings people into our life that help give us clarity and confidence in that calling. God has used Tim throughout our ministry and we know that *Fit and Flourish* will help you develop confidence and clarity in the wonderful calling God has given you."
--Pastor Dylan and Aubrey Does, Restore Church, Marshalltown, Iowa

"Whether you are a ministry veteran or someone who is simply trying to find your place in serving God, *Fit and Flourish* is a tool you can't afford to be without. Tim Roehl combines practical tools and exercises with heart-felt spiritual guidance in a way that creatively challenges a person to find their ministry sweet spot. As you read and reflect, your heart will be warmed to passionately pursue God's purpose in your life. Tim's heart for Christian leaders shines through as he coaches through the written word!"
--Rev. Dave Dignal, Pastor, Adjunct Professor, Indiana Wesleyan University

"My friend and colleague Tim Roehl has a passion for Jesus and for helping people live in the fullness of the promises of God. A life that is fit according to these promises will flourish in the joys of life. As I read these pages I understood this is not the promise of an easy life. Just the opposite. It's the challenge of the Apostle Paul to be all that Christ saved you to be."
--Dr. David Long, Vice President of Theological Development, One Mission Society, Inc.

"Dr. Tim Roehl helps people develop the understanding and skills essential to thrive as they live out God's calling on their lives. In this book, he draws from his years of study and experience to come alongside readers in a very practical, insightful way so that they can fit and flourish!"
--Dr. Bob Fetherlin, President, One Mission Society, Inc.

"Many Christians are ineffective in ministry because they're simply in the wrong spot, trying to carry on a ministry that God never intended for them. If you are wondering, "Where is my place in

God's Kingdom?", this book is for you. Dr. Tim Roehl offers simple, practical coaching that will enable you to see God, yourself and the world more clearly. This book is a road map to finding your most effective place for serving God. I recommend it for college students, young ministers or anyone who feels there is something more they can do to advance God's Kingdom."
--Lawrence W. Wilson, author of *The Long Road Home* and blogger at www.lawrencewilson.com

Tim has taken his years of experience of helping followers of Christ find their sweet spot, what he calls "fit and flourish," and has condensed his process into a single volume. Tim's masterful use of word pictures allow us to better understand that God has created each of us uniquely and for a divine purpose in his Kingdom. His stylized usage of alliteration and acronyms creates memorable tools so the reader can easily remember Scriptural principals. Tim's insights show that when a person discovers how God designed them to fit into God's master plan, they will flourish and thrive beyond their wildest dreams, not for themselves, but for the sake of fulfilling God's call upon their lives to help complete the Great Commission.
--Jason and Lora Campbell, Directors of One Mission Kids, One Mission Society

Foreword

There is something special about people from the upper Midwest. Tim is from Minnesota. I am from northern North Dakota. This is important.

My wife Julie and I had joined a mission organization called *Church Resource Ministries* back in the 1990's, and it has remained our home now for nearly 25 years. Early on, though, I did not find a sense of fit among our peers in this entrepreneurial bunch. As I got to know Tim and Shirley Roehl, fellow CRM missionaries from the Midwest, we discovered that CRM was, in our estimation, a "southern California culture" which was different than our Great Plains heritage and values.

Together we realized that we would have to contextualize to have influence; that is, we would have to figure out how to *find our place* and *have impact*. Thus began a wonderful friendship of over 20 years. It was here that I experienced my first lesson in Tim's heartbeat to help others *fit and flourish*!

Who is this *Fit & Flourish* maestro? Well, for starters he is a *man of Alliteration*. Give Tim a set of words—any words on any subject—and he will make it flow with a set of "c's" or row of "g's" that will make the concept or application sing. Whether it is GROW or PROMISE, tools you will find herein, Tim not only makes sense with words. He also makes them memorable!

Tim is a *man of Analysis*. He has an insatiable desire to understand how things and people work. He has made asking questions into in art form. In fact, I credit Tim Roehl as the first person who really taught me to ask people really good coaching questions about who they are, how they function, and much, much more.

Tim is also a *man of Affinity*. He gives high priority to relationship. I have watched Tim and Shirley love people into the Kingdom in their neighborhood. We have observed them loving and serving their children and grandchildren. I have been privileged, with other teammates on our *Grip Birkman Global Resource Team,* to experience Tim's playing his faithful part in so many different ways and over an extended period of years. He is one of the few people in my life who *always* seeks to pursue and value me personally, even setting up coaching calls with me—a trait and model for which I will be forever grateful.

But my brother and Kingdom partner is also a *Gospel man*. Everything about this guy oozes the Gospel and sharing the story of Jesus is never far from Tim in his relationships or his writing. His present work with One Mission Society has extended that passion even farther around the world.

He is a *Gracious man* as well. Not only does he represent those of us who claim Midwestern roots and Midwestern manners, but he graciously pursues, asks questions and values every person he meets—and no, I am not exaggerating.

But Tim is also strategic when showing grace as a *body life Gardener.* His desire to cultivate meaning and application into people's lives as seekers, new Christians, teammates, pastors, church planters, and missionaries – both for themselves and for others they reach.

That is a bit about the person of Tim Roehl. One other thing, though, reflects the heart of this book. When you combine Tim's heart for Jesus, people and analysis, what you get in a tool like *Fit and Flourish* are great questions! Here are some of those questions you will find in the following pages which will tempt you wider and deeper into its content:

> What is transformissional leadership?
> How do you contribute on a team?
> Who inspires you, and how?
> Which voice are you listening to?
> Who do you need to forgive?
> What does it mean to live supernaturally as an eagle?

Tim, "Uff-da" to you, Brother! May you fit and flourish as you continue to steward your Kingdom part and your Body Life relationships. And blessings to all who read, alliterate and analyze this gracious, Gospel-focused, body life gardening content.

—Dr. Paul R. Ford, Body Life specialist, Pioneer of the Grip Birkman process, *Church Resource Ministries*

The Call

At first it was a gentle whisper, inviting me...audible but not quite discernable. Instinctively I leaned forward, listening intently. I knew that Voice! He was saying something new, but not completely clear.

I could sense an unseen Hand slowly and steadily beckoning me in a direction I could understand but a destination I couldn't...at least not yet. My heart turned to the invitation as if drawn by an invisible magnet.

It was a divine invitation...a summons to prepare...a *call*. There was a sense of destiny in the invitation...and something in me began to burn.

He was pointing me toward something that didn't apply to my current situation, and it seemed to be way beyond me. My heart felt an odd mixture of apprehension and exhilaration. There was a sense of eager delight about the direction, but uncertainty about the destination... what was He up to?

Slowly, I began to see how intentional He was in His purposes. The gentle whisper increased in intensity and clarity. The fire began to burn more brightly. Seemingly unconnected circumstances began to fit a cohesive pattern. "Chance" meetings with certain people began to bear the unmistakable imprint of divine appoint-ments. Particular books and other media spoke deeply to me, adding fuel to the flame of a sense of destiny. Life experiences that left me at times heartbroken and at other times bursting with joy came at key times...as if unseen Hands were forming my character from a master plan. He was stretching me, sharpening me, impressing on me issues that all centered in my heart. It was then that I realized His ultimate goal was to make me like

Him. No matter what else the call might mean...it had to flow from a heart He had cleansed and filled...a heart like His. I yielded completely, lest anything in my life corrupt the call.

He answered my cry for cleansing with grace beyond my greatest heart desires and needs.

As He continued to work on me, the plan was coming into focus...and I was shaken to realize how big His purposes were. I had thought this was about me...but He had so much more in mind! It was about multitudes of people influenced for His Kingdom...multitudes living in the valley of decision waiting for someone to lead them to the forgiveness of the Father purchased with the blood of His Son. I couldn't believe He would allow me to be a part of something so awesome and eternal. I was humbled again, overwhelmed with inadequacy.

His response was to remind me again of His overwhelming adequacy and sufficiency.

As I had many times before, I could only bow before Him in grateful awe, thankful that He had chosen me to be a small part of such a master plan so full of wonder.

Slowly I was able to acknowledge that He had made no mistake in choosing me...but the period of preparation took much longer than I could have imagined. He was willing to take the time to do the job right even though I questioned His methods more often than I'd want to admit now.

The call became clear, as if He had written it indelibly on my heart. I was sharing the call, and found confirmation from other members of His family. The fire was burning hot, the urge to step into the fullness of His purposes intense and insistent. Something inside of me was restless, sensing an impending change. He had taught me to be grateful and faithful for where I was, but my heart had the uncomfortable, radiant, exhilarating expectancy of someone eight and half months spiritually pregnant.

When would He bring the birth?

It wouldn't be long now...or so I thought. I think He just smiled and continued His specially tailored preparation. I wondered if I would ever be ready. He was just waiting for a moment in time He'd designed before I was even born.

Finally...on an ordinary day from my perspective and a day of destiny from His...

He opened the door.

Suddenly everything made supernatural sense. What had started as a gentle whisper of invitation was now a consuming passion. All the preparation...the tapestry of life experiences He wove so carefully and skillfully together...now I could *see* it! There before me was the open door...

He smiled and reached out to me...inviting me to walk with Him into the fullness of the call. I could see it all now...the invitation...the preparation...this was the culmination. This is what He made me for! A sense of destiny was at last becoming reality.

I took His hand...and walked through the door.

--Tim Roehl

1

The Call to Fit and Flourish

"To be or not to be. That is the question." (Shakespeare's Hamlet)
To be what? That's my question. (The rest of us)

"Fit and flourish"...

Think about a time in your life when those words were true of you. What words describe that time?

I've asked that question of thousands of people. Their answers have been varied, powerful and creative. Along with the words they used, the tone of their voices and their body language spoke even more powerfully. "Fit and flourish" always generates thoughtful, positive, hopeful, enthusiastic responses.

If "fit and flourish" is a new phrase to you, I'm not surprised. I'm a "words" guy, so creating fresh ways to say things comes naturally to me. The phrase "fit and flourish" came naturally when I first created it. Perhaps it found me more than I found it. It's been amazing to me how that phrase resonates with so many people. It rings true to them and taps into inner longings, generating energy, hope and faith.

You may have heard similar expressions of fit and flourish...

I found my *"sweet spot."*

Athletes describe being *"in the zone"* when they are playing at their best helping their team win.

One person said, *"Life is not measured by the number of moments we breathe, but the number of moments that take our breath away."*

Many of us have come home from a long day of "fit and flourish" work or ministry, exhausted yet energized. We look heavenward and say, *"I was made for this...thank You, God!"*

Fit—"This is where I belong! This is my place and these are my people."

Flourish—"This is what God created me for! This is where I can make the biggest difference for His glory."

Fit and flourish is not so much defined as described. You know it when you experience it. You also know when you don't.

Many surveys have been done asking people about their satisfaction quotient. One survey done by Deloitte's Shift Index survey quoted in Business Insider's website found that 80% of people are unhappy with their work, saying people are now "picking passion over a paycheck every time."[1] Corey Keyes, a psychology researcher, says that only twenty percent of Americans flourish, while up to one third languish, which she describes as people who describe their lives as hollow or empty.[2]

In her great book "Made to Flourish: Beyond Quick Fixes to a Thriving Organization," Shelly Trebesh notes that God created us to flourish. In Genesis 1:11, 20, 26 and 28 we learn that God made us in His own image to share His life with us. He gave us His creation to care for so it will flourish. He blessed us and commanded us to be fruitful and multiply. In Isaiah 61, the Lord gives us spiritual anointing to bring good news of His love, favor, deliverance and provision to the whole world. In Revelation 21:3,4 we see the culmination of His restoring love through Jesus by taking us home to Him, bringing eternal victory over sin and death. People from every nation find their ultimate fit and flourish with Him in eternity!

So...what are you passionate about? What makes life worth living? Where do *you* fit and flourish?

That's a very personal question. It also can sound like an "it's all about me" question. It can become very easy for fit and flourish to shrink down to a little self-contained world. That would be selfish, tragic and pointless. Still, starting with "me" is the beginning of understanding the true scope of fit and flourish.

What does fit and flourish look like in a "me" context?
"Fit and flourish" is not just a descriptive phrase, it portrays a deep yearning in people's lives. Created in God's very own incredible image, we were made for more than just trying to achieve the typical dream of having a family, financial security, health, safety and comfort...a *nice* life. We were made for more than "nice"! God made us for more than just to survive...more than nice and safe...He made us to thrive...to fit and flourish! He made us to discover and live out His unique, eternal, supernatural Kingdom dream for each of us...a Kingdom dream that makes life worth living in the here-and-now with a view toward the hereafter....a life secure in unconditional love—a life of overflowing generosity, grace, risk, sacrifice, adventure, discomfort, abundance—a "bigger than me" life that can't be lived without a big God.

Trebesh adds, "When we flourish, we experience emotional, psychological and social well-being. We are full of life—peaceful, cheerful, satisfied and productive. We accept ourselves as we are, knowing our strengths and weaknesses. We engage challenges, enjoy learning and embrace an overall sense of purpose. We expect our days to be useful and hopeful. Flourishing people have strong relationships and connectedness to community, contributing as well as receiving...sound like what God might intend life to be?"[3]

So, let me expand that question further...

What does fit and flourish look like in a "we" context?
Life is meant to be lived in the realm of relationships. God made us for community...for family...for team...the "me" is always in the context of the "we." Trebesh, who works with ministry organizations around the world, gives this powerful description:

"Flourishing organizations are thrilling in that they pursue meaningful, kingdom-of-God-oriented purposes. They make a difference in society and individual lives. A called community that participates in God's mission is unique. The way it participates in the kingdom and partners with God for kingdom purposes is as individual as human beings themselves, and it must live uniqueness to demonstrate the full breadth of God's image. Ultimately, Christian organizations should be flourishing and thriving because that reflects their Creator's image.

Flourishing organizations are vibrant, reproducing kingdom-of-God communities called together to live in God's reign and join God's mission to proclaim and live in His kingdom and to, by God's enabling grace, pursue their unique, God-given purpose and produce God's vision of the future while creating an environment where individuals thrive. Flourishing organizations are fun, satisfying, safe environments in which individuals are restored and embrace transformation into the image of Christ. They live the authentic Jesus life—attractive, joyful, contagious."[4]

What does fit and flourish look like in a "they" context?
"They" are the people who currently exist without a personal relationship with Jesus. By most counts, over two-thirds of the people on our planet don't know Him. Without Jesus, we only exist in a physical sense. In Jesus, we not only can live an abundant life now, we can live with Him forever. We share His supernatural, eternal Life! Fit and flourish always includes a relationship with Jesus and knowing our part in helping others know Him, too.

What does fit and flourish look like in a "Him" context?
In the end, a fit and flourish life is an overflow of God's life in and through us...and He gets all the glory. It is a wonderful thing to live in such a way that when others watch us, they can only give Jesus all the credit for who we are, what we do and the difference we make. The Bible resounds with truths like these...

"And in whatever you do, do it all for the glory of God..."
(I Corinthians 10:31, NIV)

"Love the Lord your God with all your heart, soul, mind and strength and your neighbor as yourself..." (Mark 12:30-31, NIV)

"...Christ in you, the hope of glory." (Colossians 1:27, NIV)

"The thief comes to steal, kill and destroy. I have come to give you life, and life more abundantly...life to the full." (John 10:10, ESV, NIV)

If you are longing for a fit and flourish life, then I invite you to go on a journey to discover and experience what fit and flourish looks like for you.

God's Invitations to the Journey

At one point in my life, I lived with a particular verse that described my longing...and also encouraged me with invitations from the Lord:

"Stand at the crossroads and look...
   Ask for the ancient paths,
      Ask where the good way is...
         Walk in it and
            You will find rest for your souls..." (Jeremiah 6:16, NIV)

Another version expresses it this way...

> *"You are standing at the crossroads. So consider your path. Ask where the old, reliable paths are. Ask where the path is that leads to blessing and follow it. If you do, you will find rest for your souls..."* (NET)

Let's look more closely at this wonderful verse...in it we find invitations, directions and promises!

"Stand"

Take a stand for something...be solid and firm in what really matters. Stand up and pay attention to what God is saying. Stand and present yourself as you are being appointed for something great. Stand still and stop doing other things. Stand up and be noticed …come on the scene and make your best contribution.

Stand. If we are going to discover where we fit and flourish, we first have to stop long enough for us to pay attention to what God is saying to us and what He's doing in us. Many of us fill our lives with so much "noise" and busyness it's hard to hear anything. Socrates is quoted as saying *"The unexamined life is not worth living."* How willing are you to stop, take a stand and examine yours?

"…at the crossroads…" Life is full of choices. God's given everyone the gift of free will. How we choose to exercise our ability to choose on a moment by moment basis becomes the path we follow, our rhythm of life and ultimately our destiny. At different times in our lives, we will feel like we are standing at a significant crossroad. Which road you take is up to you…and it matters.

"…and look…" "Look"—lean forward, watch and listen intently for what's coming over the horizon toward you. There's an intentness, intensity and an eagerness in our watching. We really want to "see" and "hear" God's best for us! Finding where we fit and flourish will require focused discernment that resists distractions and easier detours. In this book, we'll pay attention to seven "looks" that will help you see what God's fit and flourish looks like. How willing are you to both "stand" and also "look"?

"Ask…" God is inviting us! One of my favorite definitions of prayer from Martin Luther is *"Prayer is not overcoming God's reluctance, but laying hold of His willingness."* [5] Knowing God wants us to ask Him for His best sets the stage for discovering His best. In this book, we'll ask you a number of questions that will help you in turn ask the Lord for His answers.

"…for the ancient paths (where the old reliable paths are)…" It's normal for us to feel like no one has ever gone through what we are experiencing. It's reassuring to find that others down through the generations have had the same questions, struggles, joys, fears and revelations that we do. As we walk through our fit and

flourish discernment process, we'll find the timeless, universal principles and truth that every person who's walked with the Lord came to understand and apply. If you want to fit and flourish, you'll travel a well-worn road walked by many great men and women of God throughout history! You're in good company!

"...ask where the good way is (the path that leads to blessing)" The *"good"* way is agreeable...pleasant...excellent....glad... prosperous...joyful...valuable...beneficial. God's good path is unique, customized and personalized for each person. Not only is God's fit and flourish path universal and timeless, it is also unique and timely! He designed you and your fit and flourish road very purposefully. Many times I have claimed the promise of Psalm 32:8: *"I will lead you in the way that you should go. I will instruct you and guide you along the best pathway for your life; I will advise you and watch your progress."* (NIV, LB)

"...walk in it, and you will find rest for your souls." Here is an invitation, a choice and a promise. If we will choose to walk in the way God has designed for us, we *will* find rest for our souls. "Walking" is a step by step, choice by choice, day by day, way-of-life journey. It's taking God's fit and flourish road and staying on it. In the end, we'll find it was by far the best way we could have chosen. Others will notice, be influenced by us, and thank us. Some will choose to follow us on the Jesus Road. We'll get to help others find out where they fit and flourish. When we get home to heaven, hearing the final "well done" from our Heavenly Father will be the ultimate reward.

"But you said, 'We will not walk in it." God has a fit and flourish life prepared for you. You can choose to go that way...or you can choose to say no. Choices have consequences. Choose God's best...don't miss it!

"Stand....look...ask...walk...find..." The verbs of Jeremiah 6:16 summarize our fit and flourish discernment journey. As a pastor and missionary who has assessed, coached and trained people from over 75 nations, I've had the privilege of helping thousands

of people discover what fit and flourish looks like for them. People may come from many backgrounds, but at our heart level, we're the same because we're all made in our Father's image!

With those invitations, directions and promises of Jeremiah 6:16 in mind, let's go on our discovery journey...

We'll ask the key fit and flourish questions...
    We'll look at truths and principles that make a fit and flourish life possible...
        We'll help you coach yourself forward, making your fit and flourish steps doable and practical...

Start with the Lord and how wonderful **HE** is...

Realize He made you and **ME** for unique and special purposes...

Appreciate that He placed you and me into a **WE** community of relationships...

Together, let's **SEE** His great redemptive purposes and how we each fit into them...

Walk with Him...and experience a fit and flourish life of **WHEE**!

He...Me...We...See...Whee!

2

Look Up

Say Yes to God's Invitations

For years he'd been drifting...forty years.

From the outside you would have never noticed. He went to work every day, raised his family, and was well liked in his community. For most people, that was considered a pretty good life...on the outside.

But it was on the inside, where no one could see, that he was drifting. Day followed day, week followed week and most of the time he drifted along in comfortable complacency. There were times when memories from his past rose to the surface and he struggled to shake them off. There were times where he felt an odd sense of restlessness in his spirit...as if there had to be more to his life, but he just didn't know what "more" was. Still, he didn't look much past the immediate future, because there was no greater purpose or sense of destiny that beckoned him onward and upward.

One day...an average day from all outward indications ...God broke into his life in an extraordinary way. The Creator King of the Universe ignited an ordinary bush and then lit up his heart with a vision so clear and bright that it changed him for the rest of his life... and in turn changed the course of millions of other lives.

At first he struggled to understand what God was saying, then struggled to believe that God could actually use an average guy who couldn't talk very well to fulfill a supernatural plan that was going to change the course of two nations...and ultimately world history. After reassurances from God that ranged from irritated to intimate, he finally put himself completely in the King's hands...and stepped into the greatest adventure of his life.

From a drifting man to a divinely mandated leader... what made the difference for Moses? A call...a call from a God he could trust and follow anywhere. When God puts His hand on a man or woman's life and speaks destiny to them, nothing is ever the same again. Such is the power of vision born in the heart of God and reborn in the heart of a leader cleansed, filled and yielded to the King of the Universe.

--Tim Roehl

How do you "see" God?

"If I say yes to God, I'm afraid He will...
send me to _____,
tell me to _____,
take away my _____,
make me _____"
(People describing why it's hard to say yes completely to God)

"I heard You in the garden, and I was afraid...so I hid." (Adam in Genesis 3:10)

"The thief comes only to steal, kill and destroy. I have come to give you life, and life more abundantly." (Jesus in John 10:10)

Discovering a fit and flourish life always begins with God. More importantly, with how we *see* God. In fact, any possibility of a fit and flourish life depends on our view of God because it makes all the difference in our relationship (or lack of one) with Him.

It All Started in the Garden...Two Views and Two Voices

The importance and implications of how we view God started in Eden...it all goes back to the Garden! In the Garden, we hear two voices telling us about God that give us two very different views of Him. We've been influenced by those voices and views ever since.

God's View...God's Voice
In the beginning, God told us about Himself so that we could know Him, love Him, trust Him and walk with Him. Let's listen in and learn about who He really is...

"God said...and it was so." God is <u>great.</u> (Genesis 1:1-27, KJV) Consider the greatness of God! He merely spoke, and the universe came into being. The immensity, majesty, beauty, variety, energy, intricacy and creativity of all of creation comes from Him. On top of all that, He made us as men and women in His very image. We are the crowning achievement of His creation!

"...it was good..." God is good (Genesis 1:10, 12, 18, 25, 31). Whatever God does is good because His very nature is good. Consider the goodness of God! *"He does all things well..."* (Mark 7:37)

"He blessed them...be fruitful...increase...I give..." (Genesis 1:28-30, 2:22) God is a Generous Giver. God delights in sharing His abundance with us. He gave us His world to enjoy and steward. He gave us each other to share His joy in relationship. Consider the generosity of God!

"God saw all...and it was very good." (Genesis 1:31) God's gracious goal is to share His nature with us, enjoy a relationship with us, conform us to His image and bless us so we can bless others! We are the highest joy in all His creation!

Later, when He has to deal with the consequences of Adam and Eve's sinful choices to choose their will over His will, He still makes a way for people snake-bit by sin to return to a reconciled relationship with Him. He provided a Savior Who not only crushed the snake but gave His own blood as the antidote for the poison of sin! The very first promise of God's Good News of salvation for humanity is found in Genesis 3:15, often called "the first good news," which looks ahead to what Jesus would do for the descendants of Adam and Eve. He said to the serpent,

> "And I will put enmity (open hostility)
> between you and the woman,
> And between your seed (offspring) and her Seed;
> He shall [fatally] bruise your head,
> and you shall [only] bruise His heel." (AMP)

When we see God as great, good, generous and gracious, the result can be a relationship of loving trust with Him and abundant generosity toward others. When that's true, we don't *have* to do His will, we *get* to do His will.

The Serpent/Thief's View....Voice (Genesis 3:1-5)

If there had been only that one true Voice and one view in the Garden to give us perspective on who God is, everything would be for different for everyone. But, another voice was heard in the Garden that gave a completely opposite view of God.

"Now the Serpent was more cunning...crafty....shrewd...he said..." (Genesis 3:1, KJV, NET, EBR)

"Did God really, actually say...?" (Genesis 3:1, NIV, ISV)

"That's not true! You will not surely die...." (Genesis 3:4, TEV)

"God knows that when you eat of it your eyes will be opened... you'll be like God..." (Genesis 3:5, NIV)

In that conversation with Eve, the serpent presented a different view of God...
God is not great.
God is not good.
God's a taker, not a giver.
He doesn't want what's best for you.
You can't trust Him.

Satan the serpent thief also has a goal. His goal is to get people to be afraid of a God they don't want to trust. In not trusting God, they would look somewhere else for their source of life and give their worship to someone else. Satan wants to assume God's place in our worship...and Satan is everything God is not.

Eve and Adam made a choice to listen to the serpent's voice, believe his deceptive lies about God and live as if God could not be trusted. They decided their will and way was better than His. When they did, sin entered and separated us from Him. With sin, humanity was now living under a curse. Sin and its curse bred lack of trust...selfishness...scarcity...stinginess...robbing glory from God. The result: practical atheism. "Believe in God, but behave as if He doesn't exist...because you can't really trust Him." Even people who believe in God still struggle to trust Him.

In bringing life down to its core choices, we choose between two voices and two views of God. How we "listen" is influenced by...

The way other people modeled for us how they saw God...
Life experiences...
Education about God...or lack of it...
Satan speaking his original lies, alienating us from God...
God's Spirit speaking eternal truth, inviting us back to God...

If we choose to listen to God's voice and embrace the true view of Him, a fit and flourish life is possible.

If we choose to listen to the thief's voice and accept a false premise of God, finding a fit and flourish life will always be a struggle if not impossible. We'll try to draw life from a substitute for the Lord, which becomes an idol. Whether that idol is our-selves, our possessions, our positions, our popularity, our power or something else, we'll come up empty, dry, deceived, defeated and depleted.

Which voice are you listening to?

Voices

I hear them calling: *"Hey, you....come 'ere."*

From a distance they make promises.

They promise love...
   ...to satisfy needs to be accepted and belong.

They promise light...
   ...to give guidance and clarity in the darkness.

They promise life...
   ...to help me scale the heights to success and
significance.

But...the closer I get to the idol voices, the more I come
to understand:

Idols are liars.

The guiding light they promise is deception worse than
the blind leading the blind. Idols intentionally lead me
further down into the darkness of deceit and despair.
The clarity they promise leads only to confusion and
ultimately to chaos.

Idols are lechers.
   They promise love *to* me...
      unconditional love
      easy love
      tolerant love.

But...in reality what they really want is to demand love
from me--their only goal was my worship, allegiance
and addiction. Their tender glances and gentle caresses
turn into lustful leering...hands pawing me, molesting

me. They take my love first by my own volition but ultimately by violence.

Their love is warped—fiendish in its deceptiveness and deceit. Their intention was only to draw me in with the promises of love and then plunge me into their perverted, self-saturated black hole and leave me destroyed.

Idols are leeches.

Sometimes I found they had attached themselves so subtly to the skin of my spirit that I hadn't realized they had really gotten under the skin and were drawing jugular life. The very thing they promised me--the gusto lusts of life that promised to set me high on the mountain of success and at last show me my significance from its lofty perch--that very thing had been leeching life from me all along.

The pinnacle was barren...
    meaningless...
        lifeless.

I finally saw the idols for what they are:
depraved monsters with demonic whispers behind them. They promise I can have it all but take me for everything I have instead.

My heart wants to throw up, horrified by
    the sickening stench behind the sweet words...
        the hideous face behind the seductive mask.

I am repulsed.

I am rocked to the core by the fact that I ever listened to them in the first place, much less tried to find life from them.

I repent.

There's Another Voice calling....

This Voice is different than any other I've ever heard. At first I hear the Voice calling *my* name.
    As I turn to the Voice,
        I see the Face.

What a Face! There is no mask on this Face. He looks at me with eyes that see all... knows all there is to me--even behind my masks. I can see in His eyes there is both complete knowing....and complete love.

Then I see His hands--He's reaching out to me--and I see the horrific scars...nail pierced evidences of love.

He says quietly, "For you...because I love you. You are worth everything to Me."

I can't take my eyes off His nail-scarred hands.

What I see rocks me to the core again. How could I be such a fool to have tried to find love anywhere but from Him? All I had given the idols mocked the love He so freely gave and rightfully deserved. I am rocked to the core...by grace.

I repent again in tears---not only to turn from the liar idols but to turn to my Jesus, my Living Lord.

My tears don't obscure my view of Him--they make Him all the more clear. Then He smiles at me....and speaks again. *"Come, child, come."*

Tentatively, tearfully I take a step--right into His waiting arms and His grace-filled embrace. He calls me by my name again, tenderly. I lay my head on His broad shoulder and rest in His strong arms.

I rest.
  Secure.
    Complete.
      Whole.

He had promised me nothing--He had just called my name and let me see His face and the Cross-induced evidences of His love.

He had simply called me to come to Him.

Yet, standing there in His arms--
  all the promises my heart longed for came true!

Light...love...life...they were in *Him* all along.

I still hear the idol voices calling sometimes, especially in my times of weakness, darkness and dryness...too often still I turn my heart to listen.

But now I hear the Voice of Another...
  I see the Face of Grace
    I feel the strong arms of unconditional love.
      I know the piercing price He paid.

I turn to Him...the only Voice I need.

Lord Jesus, I know You are holding me more closely than I can ever hold You. As long as I am with You, I have everything my heart needs and infinitely more.

Hold me closer, Lord.

--Tim Roehl

How do you "see" God's will and calling?

"Oh, my brothers and sisters! Look at how good God is! When you see how merciful He's been to us, you'll want to give yourself completely to Him...go all in! It's the only reasonable thing we can do! You won't let the world squeeze you into its mold anymore—you'll ask God to transform you from the inside out by giving you a whole new attitude toward life. With that attitude, you'll discover God's will for you...not just good, not just pleasing, but perfect. You'll say, 'He made me for this!'" (Romans 12:1, 2, Tim Roehl)

"So here's what I want you to do, God helping you: Take your everyday, ordinary life—your sleeping, eating, going-to-work, and walking-around life—and place it before God as an offering. Embracing what God does for you is the best thing you can do for him. Don't become so well-adjusted to your culture that you fit into it without even thinking. Instead, fix your attention on God. You'll be changed from the inside out. Readily recognize what he wants from you, and quickly respond to it. Unlike the culture around you, always dragging you down to its level of immaturity, God brings the best out of you, develops well-formed maturity in you. I'm speaking to you out of deep gratitude for all that God has given me, and especially as I have responsibilities in relation to you. Living then, as every one of you does, in pure grace, it's important that you not misinterpret yourselves as people who are bringing this goodness to God. No, God brings it all to you. The only accurate way to understand ourselves is by what God is and by what he does for us, not by what we are and what we do for him. (Romans 12:1-3, The Message)

"Follow Me, and I will make you fishers of men." (Matthew 4:19 KJV)

You've been taking time to focus on how you see God and how you see yourself. Processing those two issues first allows us to begin looking at all the other issues in discovering a fit and flourish life.

Now, what's your understanding of what God's will and calling are—what He wants you to be and do?

For some people, God's will and God's call (I'm using them interchangeably in our fit and flourish process) are scary.

We're afraid God's going to ...
    ask us to do something we don't want to do,
      go somewhere we don't want to go, or
        give up something we don't want to give up.

Our attitude is often "I *have* to do God's will." It's done with a sense of duty or obligation to a demanding God...forced to choose something we really don't want to do.

Guess where that response is coming from? You're right!

A false view of God...
  A false view of self...
    A selfish will that says to God, "MY will be done, not Yours."

For others of us, God's will and God's call are a surprising, humbling and delightful invitation. So grateful for His mercy, we are thrilled that God would invite us to...

Do things we never dreamed we could do.
  Have influence we never dreamed we could have.
   Help more people than we ever dreamed we could help.
   Go places we never dreamed we could go.
    Glorify God beyond what we dreamed was possible.

God's call is far beyond our personal ability, which makes us all the more dependent on Him. But because we know He loves us, that He's good, generous, gracious and wants what's best for us and for His greater purposes, we trust and follow Him.

We don't *have* to follow God's call, we *get* to do God's will!

In fact, the meaning of the word "will" found in Romans 12:2, Ephesians 5:17 and I Thessalonians 4:3 has the idea that God's will is God's desire, inclination or pleasure for us personally, and ultimately part of the way that He wants to bless the whole world. God's will is not always easy, but when we live with eternity in mind, we find our greatest joy and contribution when we say "yes" unreservedly to Him.

George Mueller, one of the great heroes of faith in the 1800's, is quoted as saying, *"Ninety percent of knowing God's will is being willing to do it, no matter what it is."*

One of my life principles is, *"There is no sweeter, secure and super-natural place than living in the center of God's will."*

Many people struggle with the question, "How can I know God's will for me?" Perhaps you've already noticed that the more important questions before we get to that one are...

How do you "see" God?
How do you "see" yourself?
How do you "see" God's will?

Once you've addressed those questions with truth, grace and willingness, you are ready to learn about the "how" of God's calling.

Let's look at some principles of how God calls...

1. His call *starts* with His invitation that is always expressed in two main dimensions as found in Matthew 4:17-19 and Mark 1:17-18:

    "<u>Follow</u> Me"—we're called to walk with and become like Him. The early church fathers used to describe this as our "first order calling"...our first calling is to Him! Jesus calls us to be with Him...a calling to relationship, to *being.*

    "I will make you <u>fishers</u> of men"—to work with Him for His great redemptive purposes in our world! The early church fathers portrayed this as our "second order calling"...joining Him on His mission. We get to be part of what God's up to...a call to *doing.* God's universal calling--His will for all of us—can be described in the simplest of terms as *follow* and *fish.*

2. He *speaks* to us in different ways, but personalizes His call in ways that are intimate and *sacred.* His call is universal (follow and fish), but also very unique and personal!

Consider how His call came to different people in the Bible:
- Moses: a dramatic experience on an ordinary day, a burning bush experience (Exodus 3)
- Gideon: in weakness and confirming signs (Judges 6)
- Jonah: scary and persistent because he was resistant (Jonah)
- Isaiah: a supernatural revelation accompanied by sanctifying power (Isaiah 6)
- Andrew: a simple invitation—"Come, and you will see" (Matthew 4)
- Peter: humbled and overwhelmed by a boat load of fish (Luke 5)
- Paul: blinded by the Light (Acts 9)
- Barnabas and Paul: with others during a church service (Acts 13)
- Elijah: the Spirit's still small voice while hiding out in a cave (I Kings 18)

At One Mission Society (OMS), we do a wonderful exercise as part of our "One Weekend" experience to help people explore what God's calling might be. Here are some of the ways that were discovered together about how God calls at a particular One Weekend:
- His Word, either personally or through the messages of others
- Others' example or invitation
- Open doors
- As part of a team or family call
- Miracles
- Visions, dreams
- A growing sense of burden
- An outgrowth of natural skills and experiences
- In prayer and worship

- Unexpected times, ways and places
- Recognizing how His gifts operate with His power, joy and fruit
- Paying attention to longings
- In solitude and silence

Our Lord is creative and amazing in how He calls! Our attitude toward Him and our willingness to trust and follow Him help us tune in to how He is speaking. Throughout the rest of our *Fit and Flourish* book, we'll look at many aspects of God's calling.

3. He *stretches, sharpens and shapes* us to fit His call. He does not call the qualified, He qualifies us to the call!
4. His call is *specific*...to a place, to particular people, to a special person (mate), to a profession or position, to His possibilities we may not even recognize yet!
5. His call is lived in *seasons* of our journey.
6. His personal call always fits into His bigger purposes. "God is always up to something *supernaturally* bigger!
7. His call *sustains*. When everything else is up for grabs, it's His call that keeps us in place and sustains us.

Coach Yourself Forward

What words would you use to describe your view of God's calling and will?

Which phrase describes you more:
   'I *have* to do God's will."
   "I *get* to do God's will."
   Why?

On a scale of 1 to 100, where 1 means, "God, leave me alone" and 100 means, "Whatever You want, Lord, I want to be in on it!," how would you rate yourself right now?

What was helpful to you when we talked about the "how" of God's calling? Why?

I Am a Soldier of God

"I am a soldier in the army of my God. The Lord Jesus Christ is my commanding officer. The Holy Bible is my code of conduct. Faith, prayer, and the Word are my weapons of warfare. I have been taught by the Holy Spirit, trained by experience, tried by adversity and tested by fire.

I am a volunteer in this army, and I am enlisted for eternity. I will either retire in this army at the Rapture or die in this army; but I will not get out, sell out, be talked out, or pushed out. I am faithful, reliable, capable and dependable. If my God needs me, I am there. If He needs me to teach the children, work with the youth, help adults or just sit and learn, He can use me because I am there!

I am a soldier. I am not a baby. I do not need to be pampered, petted, primed up, pumped up, picked up or pepped up. I am a soldier. No one has to call me, remind me, write me, visit me, entice me, or lure me. I am a soldier. I am not a wimp. I am in place, saluting my King, obeying His orders, praising His name, and building His kingdom! No one has to send me flowers, gifts, food, cards, candy or give me handouts. I do not need to be cuddled, cradled, cared for, or catered to. I am committed. I cannot have my feelings hurt bad enough to turn me around. I cannot be discouraged enough to turn me aside. I cannot lose enough to cause me to quit. When Jesus called me into this army, I had nothing. If I end up with nothing, I will still come out ahead. I will win.

My God has and will continue to supply all of my needs. I am more than a conqueror. I will always triumph. I can do all things through Christ. Devils cannot defeat me. People cannot disillusion me. Weather cannot weary me.

Sickness cannot stop me. Battles cannot beat me. Money cannot buy me. Governments cannot silence me and hell cannot handle me!

I am a soldier. Even death cannot destroy me. For when my Commander calls me from this battlefield, He will promote me to captain and then allow me to rule with Him. I am a soldier in His army, and I'm marching claiming victory. I will not give up. I will not turn around. I am a soldier, marching heaven bound.

Here I stand! Will you stand with me?

(This piece is often attributed to an unnamed African Christian leader shortly before he was martyred for his allegiance to Jesus)

How is your relationship with God?

That's always an interesting question to ask people. Quite often the answer depends on current circumstances and how a person is feeling at the moment.

However, there are some things that we can and should know for sure about our relationship with God regardless of emotional highs and lows, situational stress , success or other fleeting factors.

"...I am not in the least ashamed. For I know the One in whom I have placed my confidence, and I am perfectly certain that the work he has committed to me is safe in his hands until that day." (II Timothy 1:12 Phillips)

"These things I have written to you who believe in the name of the Son of God [which represents all that Jesus Christ is and does], so that you will know [with settled and absolute knowledge] that you [already] have eternal life." (I John 5:13, AMP)

The word "know" means we have certainty both because something is a settled fact and because of our personal experience. God wants us to *know* that we are His children—forgiven, adopted, loved, given eternal life...and so much more!

Maybe a better question is to ask, **"What does God want for me in my relationship with Him?"** Romans 12:2 reminds us that His will is good, pleasing and perfect. Ephesians 5:17 says that the Lord wants us to be wise enough to understand what His will is.

I Thessalonians 4:3 and 5:23 actually tell us what God's will and desire for us is...and it opens the door to a theme we find all through His Word.

"It is God's will that you should be sanctified...Now may the God of peace Himself sanctify you entirely; and may your spirit and soul and body be preserved complete, without blame at/ until the coming of our Lord Jesus Christ. (I Thessalonians 4:3, 5:23 NASB, NIV)

God's desire...His call...His pleasure...is to sanctify us.

"Sanctify" is not a word we hear often in everyday life, so it's important to understand its meaning. When God wants to "sanctify" us, He wants to:
 Separate us from sinful ways,
  Set us apart for a special purpose,
   Make us pure, holy and clean inside and out,
    Fill us with the Holy Spirit so He can live His life through us!

A holy God of love wants to cleanse our hearts so He can live His life of holy love through us! There are multiple pictures of that life in His Word--
   A clean heart—Psalm 51:10
   An undivided heart—Psalm 86:11
   An abundant life—John 10:10
   Holiness—Hebrews 12:14
   Partaking of and sharing His divine nature—II Peter 1:4
   Rivers of living water...an overflowing life!—John 7:37
   Free of the body of death (sinful nature)—Romans 7:24
   Dead to sin, alive to God—Romans 6:6-14
   The beautiful life—Psalm 29:2
   Filled and satisfied—Matthew 5:6
   Pure in heart, able to see God—Matthew 5:8
   A heart of flesh (tender and responsive to God)—Ezekiel 36
   The rest of faith (not living in our own strength)—Hebrews 4
   The filling of the Spirit—Acts 1:8
   Power to be His witnesses—Acts 1:8
   purified our hearts by faith (Peter's testimony)—Acts 15
   love from a pure heart (Paul)—I Timothy 1:5
   sanctified entirely...blameless—I Thessalonians 5:23
   Holy even as He is holy—I Peter 1:16-17
   Sanctified by the truth...sent like Jesus (John 17:17,18)

What a wonderful relationship God wants us to enjoy with Him! Let's look at how He does that a little more deeply...

If you are a Christian, you will have an instinctive desire to please God...an "inside out" motivation for living. Yet, many believers struggle to please God. They lack freedom, joy and power to live the abundant life God wants for us. Why? They have an internal traitor, a self-centered sinful nature, that resists God's reign in their hearts. BUT—we can be free to experience God's best for our lives and live to please Him.

The Path to a Sanctified, Overflowing, Abundant Life
(I Thessalonians 5:23, 24; Psalm 51) The sanctified life begins with a crisis point followed by a lifelong process...

1. Be *convicted* of your need for a clean heart. (Psalm 51:1-6) *"Have mercy on me, O God...according to Your great compassion, blot out my transgressions. Wash away all my iniquity and cleanse me from my sin. For I know my transgressions and my sin is always before me." (NIV)*

   Just as David recognized he needed both forgiveness for his sins/transgressions (sinful actions) and cleansing from his sin (the sinful nature that motivated his sinful actions), we also come to realize that we need God to cleanse us at the level of our heart, not just our actions.

2. *Confess* your need and desire for a clean heart that sustains a life that willingly chooses God. (Psalm 51:6-9)
   "Surely You desire truth in the inner parts (my inner man)... Cleanse me...and I will be clean; wash me, and I will be whiter than snow....grant me a willing spirit (make me willing to choose You), to sustain me." (NIV, KJV, NET)

   When we know our need, we can confess to God we are agreeing with Him about what He wants to do for us. To "confess" means to agree. In God's eyes, confession is a positive thing, because He sees us agreeing with Him! Conviction is painful, but confession is meant to be liberating.

3. *Consecrate* yourself completely to God.
   "....give me an undivided heart..." (Psalm 86:11)
   Consecration is our part...completely yielding of our right to ourselves. The last thing we let go of is the right to rule our

own life. We sign over the title deed to our life and give God permission to take full ownership of every nook and cranny from our past and every motivation and ambition for our future. We are fully His! Everything that held God back from giving us His very best is now surrendered willingly to Him.

4. Ask God to *cleanse* your heart in simple faith. (Psalm 51:9,10)
   "Create in my a clean (pure) heart, O God and renew a stead-fast (constant, resolute) spirit within me...Restore to me the joy of Your salvation and grant me a willing spirit (make me willing to choose You), to sustain me." (NIV, KJV, NET)

   Our part is giving ourselves to the Lord completely and asking Him to cleanse our hearts in simple faith. We can't make ourselves holy. When Jesus died and rose for us, He did it not only to forgive our sins, but cleanse our sinful nature so we can live aligned and allied with Him.

5. *Claim* His promise by faith and enter in! (Luke 11:13)
   "...how much more will your Father in Heaven give the Holy Spirit to those who ask Him?"

   God the Holy Spirit's part is to cleanse us and then fill our lives so that He can live through us! The work of sanctification is both a crisis and an ongoing process...when Paul shared God's desire to sanctify us in I Thessalonians 4, he also described the wonderful benefits for us. Let's look at what that transformation looks like as He fills us and lives through us.

The Power of a Sanctified, Overflowing, Abundant Life
(I Thessalonians 4:3-10, 5:16-22) The Holy Spirit gives purity and authority growing in maturity in many ways...

1. *Purity* and humility (4:3-5, 6, 8, 12)
   "It is God's will that you should be holy, that you should avoid sexual immorality...learn to control your body in a way that is holy and honorable...for God did not call us to be impure, but to live a holy life. Therefore, he who rejects this instruction does not reject man but God, Who gives you His Holy Spirit..."

In a world where sexual purity, personal humility and integrity is increasingly rare, God places a high value on these qualities...and He also provides His power to live them!

2. *Peace* in relationships (4:6,9,10)
   "...no one should wrong his brother or take advantage of him... you have been taught by God to love each other...we urge you to do so more and more...."

   A life of holy love shows up most in how we treat others.

3. *Positive* influence with others. (4:12)
   "...so that your daily life may win the respect of outsiders..."

   People would rather see a sermon about Jesus by the way we live than hear one with no supporting evidence! When our lives are fueled with holy love, others want to know how that's possible. We show and tell them Who can do it for them, too!

4. A *productive* ministry of love. (4:9,10, Psalm 51:12)
   "Then I will teach your ways to other sinners, and they—guilty like me—will repent and return to you." (LB)

   A life overflowing with holy love makes the Lord attractive to others. Just as a clean engine generates more power, a clean life fueled with holy love has a more powerful influence for God.

5. Spiritual *power* to live victoriously! (I Thessalonians 4:2; 5:16-22, Romans 8:12-15)

   "Always be joyful. Never stop praying. Be thankful in all circumstances, for this is God's will for you who belong to Christ Jesus. Do not stifle the Holy Spirit. Do not scoff at prophecies, but test everything that is said. Hold on to what is good. Stay away from every kind of evil." (NLT)

   "It stands to reason, doesn't it, that if the alive-and-present

God who raised Jesus from the dead moves into your life, he'll do the same thing in you that he did in Jesus, bringing you alive to himself? When God lives and breathes in you (and he does, as surely as he did in Jesus), you are delivered from that dead life. With his Spirit living in you, your body will be as alive as Christ's! So don't you see; we don't owe this old do-it-yourself life one red cent. There's nothing in it for us, nothing at all. The best thing to do is give it a decent burial and get on with your new life. God's Spirit beckons. There are things to do and places to go! This resurrection life you received from God is not a timid, grave-tending life. It's adventurously expectant; greeting God with a childlike, "What's next, Papa?" (Message)

"For the Kingdom of God is not a matter of eating and drinking, but of righteousness, peace and joy in the Holy Spirit, because anyone who serves Christ in this way is pleasing to God and approved by men." (Romans 14:17, 18 NIV)

"The Kingdom of God is not a matter of talk but of power."
(I Corinthians 4:20 NIV)

The life Jesus wants for us is surrendered, sanctified, satisfying, sent...step into it!

Coach Yourself Forward

As we listed many of the biblical pictures of the life God wants for us, which ones resonated most with you? Why?

What is your response to the life God wants you to experience with Him?

Have you experienced the pleasure of God's best for you...a sanctified heart? If not, come to Him now...and enter in!

Twelve Things the Holy Spirit Wants To Do For, In and Through You!

He *calls* us to experience life in God! (Romans 8:1,2 8)

He *cleanses* us from sin. (I Peter 1:2; Acts 15:8, 9; Psalm 51:10)

He *confirms* our relationship with God. (Romans 8:1, 15-17)

He *celebrates* our worth to Him, giving us joy. (Zephaniah 3:17)

He *communes* with us. (Romans 8:1; John 14:15-18)

He *counsels* and guides us with truth. (Romans 8:26-27; John 16:13-14)

He *conforms* us to the image of Christ. (Romans 8:28-30)

He *comforts* us. (John 14:26-27; II Corinthians 1:3-5)

He *corrects* us. (Romans 8:5-9)

He gives us spiritual gifts to build up His *Church*. (I Corinthians 12:4-7,11)

He *communicates* Jesus through us to others. (Acts 1:8)

He *confers* Christ's authority to *conquer* Satan, heal disease, and preach God's Good News of the Kingdom. (Luke 9:1-2)

How do you best connect with the Lord?

"I don't feel like I'm a very good Christian," my friend Kristy said. Her face showed a mixture of sadness, frustration and pain.

"Why not?" I asked.

Kristy is a wonderful young pastor's wife with two small children. "Some of the older pastor's wives I know are such deep women of God. They get up very early, read their Bibles and pray for a long time. Some even journal. I can't do that...I've got two small kids and I'm not a morning person. I'm just not spiritual like them."

I sensed it was a signature moment. "When do you feel close to God?" I asked.

Almost instantly she knew. "Oh!" her face lit up as she responded. "Music. I feel close to God when I'm playing or singing or listening to music. When the kids and I drive to school every morning, we turn worship music up loud and sing with all our hearts...and God meets us in the car."

"How about taking more time to connect with the Lord through music?" I asked.

"Can I do that?" she asked.

"Why not?" I replied. I shared with her the concepts of "God Languages" and a growing understanding showed on her face. "What might that look like for you?" I asked.

Together we coached Kristy to a way of connecting with the Lord that better fit how God made her. When our

> visit was done, there was hope in her eyes and a smile
> on her face. Such can be the power of understanding
> and applying the powerful concepts of "Spiritual
> Temperaments" or "God Languages."

When do you feel closest to God?
How do you best relate to the Lord?
What words or pictures best describe those times?

When it comes to relating to God and growing in our spiritual lives, most of us have learned some basic universal approaches and practices, such as:

Go to God in *prayer* daily
Read God's *Word* daily
O*bey* God moment by moment
W*itness* for Christ with your life and words
Trust God by *faith* for every detail of your life
Holy Spirit—let Him cleanse, fill and empower you continuously!

Although there are some universal approaches, there isn't a "one size fits all" when it comes to how we best relate to God and grow in our relationship to Him. Just as we have different personalities and spiritual gifts in the natural realm that influence our horizontal relationships, consider that we also have different spiritual temperaments that affect our vertical relationship with God. Authors Gary Thomas (*Sacred Pathways*) and Myra Perrine (*What's Your God Language?*) give us some insights in how to discern our spiritual temperaments/God languages.

A spiritual temperament or "God Language" is simply a God-given preference indicating how someone best and most naturally loves and serves God. A spiritual temperament serves as an entry point into greater awareness of Jesus...it is that place where we almost effortlessly find what some describe as our "sacred space." Understanding spiritual temperaments/God Languages can be wonderful discovery opportunities in our churches of how God has legitimately, though diversely, wired us to know Him while also displaying differing facets of His character to a watching world! While personality temperaments identify our preferences with people and the cosmos on a horizontal plane, a spiritual temperament identifies how we interact with God and the spiritual realities on a vertical level. But unlike other mere preferences, when we neglect our spiritual temperaments, we often feel dry and lifeless spiritually. The spiritual temperaments (originally developed by Gary Thomas) include:

- The Activist—loving God through confrontation with evil, standing for righteousness
- The Ascetic—loving God through solitude and simplicity
- The Caregiver—loving God through serving others
- The Contemplative—loving God through reflection and adoration
- The Enthusiast—loving God through mystery and celebration
- The Intellectual—loving God through the mind by reading and discussing deep topics
- The Naturalist—loving God through experiencing Him outdoors in His creation
- The Sensate—loving God through the senses—art, architecture, icons, incense
- The Traditionalist—loving God through ritual, symbol, sacrament, and tradition

In a very general sense, we tend to connect to the Lord best through three main ways (sometimes in combinations):

Approach	Spiritual Temperament/God Language
Head...history, reason, mind	Intellectual, Ascetic, Traditionalist
Heart...emotions, senses, expressiveness	Enthusiast, Contemplative, Naturalist
Hands...actions, service	Activist, Sensate, Caregiver

Yes, there are a variety of ways God's people love and serve Him.

So why is it so important for us to understand our spiritual wiring?

Well, for one reason, knowing our spiritual temperament helps us realize what stirs our passion for God. In that "aha" of divine discovery and intimacy, we breathe more easily in a spiritual sense. Plus, when people try to connect with God by modeling what they see others doing—such as singing worship songs enthusiastically, they sometimes end up feeling farther away from God than ever. This is because we each have a unique spiritual temperament. A one-size-fits-all spiritual formula simply doesn't work. But as we come to grasp how uniquely God has wired us, we truly feel free to communicate with Him in our own "love language," not only becoming "unstuck" in our relationship with Him, but also seeing others in a new light—one that brings greater appreciation and unity within the Body of Christ.

Isn't it interesting to know how we are spiritually wired? But it's more than interesting; it's imperative—because knowing how we connect most readily with God helps us love Him more authentically. It also enables us to appreciate those in our congregations, our families, and our small groups who are wired differently. Lightbulbs go on when we comprehend how a person is motivated spiritually to love and serve the Lord. Suddenly that church member, spouse, or child—whose questions or enthusiasm or needs or suggestions have been an irritation to us—is seen through a new lens: that of their spiritual temperament. And when we understand them better, we can embrace their unique "spiritual circuitry," allowing them to love God in fresh, sincere ways! With that freedom comes grace—the capacity to relinquish our quest to make others over in our own likeness and image.

Coach Yourself Forward

If you are interested in taking a simple version of Myra Perrine's "God Language" inventory, you can download it at www.sermoncentral.com/scdownloads/GodLanguages_Inventory.xls.

What might your primary "God language" be...what does it look like for you?

What might a secondary "God language" be...what does that look like for you?

How could you "taste" God languages that are not strong for you and learn from those experiences?

How do your God languages blend together?

How can you "make room" in your spiritual life to better relate to the Lord in the context of your "God languages"?

Take some time to develop some more personal and practical ways you can deepen your walk with the Lord and your work with Him according to your spiritual temperaments.

3

Look Back

Remember Where You've Come From

*"It's hard to drive into your future when you're
focusing on the rear view mirror all the time."*
(Recent "timeless wisdom")

*"Remember the days of old; consider the generations
long past. Ask your father and he will tell you, your
elders, and they will explain to you."*
(Deuteronomy 27:32)

*"Forget the former things; do not dwell on
the past."* (Isaiah 43:19)

*"For everything that was written in the past was
written to teach us, so that through the endurance
taught in the Scriptures and the encouragement they
provide we might have hope."* (Romans 15:4)

When you think about how looking back to your past helps you fit
and flourish now and into your future, it can be "interesting."

We are definitely shaped by our past...for better and for worse.
There are things from our past we want to bring forward and build
on, even praying that it will become woven into the fabric of future
generations. There are also issues that we want to leave behind
that need to be forgiven, forgotten, learned from and healed,
never to be repeated again. Yes, we are shaped by our past, but
we don't need to surrender to it.

The Bible tells us to remember the past in some ways and forget
the past in others. How does all this fit into our fit and flourish process?
If we want to live into our future, we have to learn from and leverage
our past.

What significant relationships have influenced you?

"Start close to home" is a good idea as we glean key insights by reflecting on our journey. Let's break it down into some simple questions...

<u>Who are the people who have most influenced your life?</u>

Prayerfully make a list of all the people who come to your mind. You might make some columns designating positive influence, negative influence or some of both.

Positive   **Some of Both**   **Negative**

How were you influenced by them?

What life lessons did you learn from them?

What qualities in their lives do you want for yourself?

What qualities do you want to avoid?

As you look back on what they've meant to you, what would you say to them now if you could?

You may want to thank some of them. Don't just say, "Thanks for all you've done for me" or "thank you for all you mean to me." Be specific about what they've done for you. Tell them *why* they mean so much to you. Share some of the qualities you have seen in them that you aspire to for yourself. Tell them a story about a time when they made a big difference in your life. If they are not alive here on earth anymore, find one of their family members and share with them why that person is so important to you. Never underestimate the power of gratitude!

One of the wonderful life lessons I learned from my dad, Giles Roehl, came on a warm summer night when I was a teen. Standing in the doorway of our garage in Sleepy Eye, Minnesota, my Dad simply said, "Son, never forget to say thank you." I've never forgotten that wisdom. I've passed it along often since and regularly practice it still. That life lesson is woven into the fabric of my life.

You may need to forgive some of them. The painful issues that require forgiveness are intensely personal. The issue of understanding and choosing biblical forgiveness is more important than we can imagine if we are to live a fit and flourish life.

If you struggle with unresolved issues of the past and forgiving others, you may need the help of wise counselors to help you do your part to forgive and heal from past issues so you are free to move into your future. The most important practical lessons I have learned about forgiving others and living free has been this process grounded in Ephesians 4:31, 32:

"Let there be no more resentment, no more anger or temper, no more violent self-assertiveness, no more slander and no more malicious remarks. Be kind to each other, be understanding. Be as ready to forgive others as God for Christ's sake has forgiven you." (Ephesians 4:31, 32 Phillips)

1. Come to the Cross and thank Jesus for forgiving you. Reflect on all that means to you. Rest in His grace.

2. In your heart, bring the person who you need to forgive and have them stand next to you at the Cross. What Jesus has done for you, He can do for them. What Jesus has done for you, *you* can do for them. Choose to forgive.

3. You will feel the peace of that choice, but it may not last long. Your will has chosen to forgive, but your emotions may not yet feel the power of that choice. *Keep choosing to forgive until your emotions catch up to your will.* It may take a while, but you will know and feel the peace that comes with forgiving someone else and leaving the rest up to a just God.

You may need to ask for forgiveness from some of them. Many struggle with their own bad decisions and sins from the past, especially those that have hurt others. Being willing to ask others for their forgiveness in ways that are honest, humble and holistic is a hard but healing process. You can do it! Whether others choose to forgive you or not, you can only do what you can do. Keep behaving in ways that rebuild trust. Keep trusting the Lord. The relational results are up to Him.

You may need to forgive yourself. Many are stranded in the mire of regret. Allow the strong, forgiving arms of our Savior lift you out of the muck of remorse and accept His forgiveness that restores, heals and reconciles. If Jesus has chosen to do this for you, who are you to tell Him that you are not worthy to be forgiven? Keep choosing to receive His wondrous pardon and both the reality and the feeling will come together. Walk in freedom!

Coach Yourself Forward

Who does the Lord want you to say, 'thank you' to? When will you do that?

What did the Lord say to you about people He wants you to forgive? What steps will you take?

What did the Lord say to you about the people you need to ask forgiveness from? What steps will you take?

What did the Lord say to you about forgiving yourself? What steps will you take?

What life experiences have influenced you?

When you take some time to review your life, some signature experiences will rise to the surface. Consider...
Where you grew up...
Who lived around you...
The expectations you lived with...
Triumphs of joy...
Times with tears of pain...
Hobbies you enjoyed...
Interests that captivated you...
Places you've been...
Teams you've been a part of...
Work environments...
Betrayal...
Blessing...
Special family remembrances...
Suffering and loss...
Success and gain...
Divine appointments...
Words of destiny spoken into your life...
Glimpses of God's fit and flourish future....

Coach Yourself Forward

What stands out to you?

What life lessons continue to shape you?

As Scripture reminds us, all of these things are part of God's intentional shaping process...sometimes painful, but always purposeful. It's all how we choose to respond. How are you responding to God's work in your life right now?

"For the time being no discipline brings joy, but may seem sad and painful; yet to those who have been trained by it, after-wards it yields the peaceful fruit of righteousness [right standing

with God and a lifestyle and attitude that seeks conformity to God's will and purpose]. So then, strengthen hands that are weak and knees that tremble. Cut through and make smooth, straight paths for your feet [that are safe and go in the right direction], so that the leg which is lame may not be put out of joint, but rather may be healed. Continually pursue peace with everyone, and the sanctification without which no one will [ever] see the Lord. See to it that no one falls short of God's grace; that no root of resentment (bitterness) springs up and causes trouble, and by it many be defiled..." (Hebrews 12:11-15, Amplified, NIV)

What do the "seasons" of your life look like?

Another part of our fit and flourish process requires that we recognize and respond wisely to the seasons of our lives.

Seasons of Nature, Seasons of Life
In the rhythm of creation itself, God designed seasons to give us variety and beauty. I've had the joy of living in places where each season is beautiful and easily recognizable. As a guy from Minnesota, I've found winter especially distinctive!

Think about how we could describe nature's seasons—and add some of your own words:

Spring: warming, increasing light, awakening, new life, emerging beauty, a time of seeding

Summer: hot, lots of light, rapid growth, expansive beauty, play, a time of weeding

Fall: cooling, decreasing light, expressive beauty, ripening, maturing, harvest, a time of reaping

Winter: cold, increasing darkness, inert beauty, hibernation, pruning, a time of sleeping

Coach Yourself Forward

Now...think about the seasons of your own life in a similar way.

What season are you in now?

How would you describe it?

What is the Lord teaching you in this season?

Seasons by Length

> *"Thank you!" The look on Jill's face and nod of recognition was emphatic and grateful.*
>
> *"What do you mean? I asked.*
>
> *She and her husband John looked at each other and then back at me. "You've asked us how long we've lived and ministered at each stop along our journey and identified that each of our seasons have been four to six years," she said. "When you just said that it might be wise for us to plan for a season of about five years before some important changes would come, it was like a light came on. Everywhere we've gone, we've been told that we should expect to spend the rest of our lives there. That's what good pastors do, we were told. But God didn't make us that way! He made us to help start new things, get them up and running, and then move on to start something again." I nodded in understanding. I could tell a huge weight had been lifted from them. They'd been set free to discern what fit and flourish meant for them in a powerful way.*

I've had similar conversations with people many times. Often an "aha" moment of realization shines in their eyes with nods of understanding as they discover a pattern about the length of their seasons. The length of our seasons are as unique as God's design for our lives...and an essential part of discerning fit and flourish.

Some people are made for short seasons of one to three years. Often they are good "starters" or "specialists" who work best for focused, intense, concise periods of time. Sometimes I've seen younger leaders appear to "bounce around" from one thing to another, not spending a lot of time at each stop. Yet, when they find their fit and flourish place, they often settle in for longer periods of time.

Some are made for longer periods of time—five, seven, even ten to fifteen years. Often they are developers—they have the ability to come into a situation that needs time for healing or time to build on a startup effort. Their patient, persistent, intentional work takes time and they are willing to balance people and task in the process.

Some are "lifers." They have the ability to stay in one place for a long time, even a lifetime. At their best they are maximizers who make ministries both effective and efficient. They love the joy of long-term relationships and the willingness to invest in one place through all the seasons and generations a lifetime of concentrated, located ministry represents.

I have great admiration for those who fit and flourish with under-standing about the length of their seasons. It took me awhile to recognize mine...up to this point each of my seasons has been a distinct ten years. I even understand the "seasons within" each ten year season. Knowing that makes a huge difference.

If you are younger, you may say, "Tim, I haven't lived long enough to figure out my seasons yet. What can I do?"

Great question! My advice is, "Look for the clues."
—How long did your family live in any given place?
—How long do you stay with things that you are passionate about?
—Which of the "starter," "developer" or "lifer" descriptions we just talked about resonated with you? Pray about it and see what the Lord says.

Coach Yourself Forward

What have your seasons been up to this point?

How long have they been?

What does that tell you about what fit and flourish might look like for you?

Seasons of Leadership

God tends to shape leaders in seasons, too. In His shaping, there are some general patterns we can recognize, but we'll find again how distinctively personal He is with each of us. In a reflective journal I wrote as part of the Arrow Leadership Program, I described my understanding of "seasons" in this way:

"Several years ago, I realized that I could identify how God has worked in my life by seeing Him at work in "seasons." Each season is unique, yet builds on and expands all the other seasons. Each season seems to have the following elements:

1. It begins with a *"summons to prepare"*—an inner sense that God is calling me to get ready for something I can't see at the moment but is part of His master plan for me. It flows from a growing sense of destiny I've had in my life for about the past twenty years.

2. It is followed by a *season of preparation* that doesn't appear to have much to do with what I am currently doing. Yet, I know I'm supposed to heed the inner summons and grow in these areas. Usually this time of preparation includes new people God wants me to meet, key books and messages and experiences of both success and brokenness. They help me in many ways.

3. At a certain point, *God opens the door* that makes all the preparation up to that point make perfect sense. As I walk through the door, He leads into a new realm of knowing Him and going deeper with Him. After a length of time that He has ordained, He will again issue another inner "summons to prepare." Another season is beginning, overlapping the season I'm living in, building on the seasons that have already been lived.[1]

When the Lord summons me to new seasons, He usually thrusts me into situations beyond my ability that require lots of "on-the-job training." I struggle and muddle along, trying to understand what God is trying to impart in and through my life. Later, He makes sure I meet a leader who is about ten years ahead of me in that area...someone who has it figured out and written down! What I learn from that leader clarifies and confirms the lessons God had been teaching me through that season. During these times a coach is especially invaluable.

When it comes to appreciating "seasons," it has been my great delight to come under the influence of Leighton Ford and Robert Clinton, both of whom have greatly inspired me. Sure enough, they have these issues much better figured out and written down! Anything both men write is invaluable for leaders who want to pay attention. Leighton's book, *The Attentive Life,* is an amazing study of the seasons of life. Clinton's book, *The Making of a Leader,* would be the first book I'd make sure every leader I coach on the inner journey reads. In his research of over seven hundred Christian leaders, he discovered some patterns which he called general development phases and specific ministry phases that leaders typically pass through in their maturing.

Clinton also looks at "seasons" from another very insightful perspective. This viewpoint looks at a leader's sense of vision in three phases:

In *Phase One,* the emerging leader is captured by the vision of someone else, often an influential and visible leader. Their vision is compelling and resonates deeply with things God is already planting in the emerging leader's life. Often the emerging leader will embrace the vision of the influential leader—joining their team, reading their books, emulating their methods and using their vocabulary.

In *Phase Two*, the emerging leader begins to notice that they would do some things differently than the vision of the influential leader. They perceive that their own gift mix, sense of call and ministry strategy are not the same as the vision they've been embracing. The leader begins to question why things are done certain ways, or why certain values and strategies are so important. They suggest that there might be better ways to accomplish the vision. It is at this point in many churches, denominations and organizations that the emerging leader's questions and suggestions are often judged by the positional leaders as being everything from irritating to insubordinate. Rather than learning from the emerging leader, they often drive them away. In many organizations with this attitude, there are large gaps of middle-aged leaders because the organization did not value their insights and give them room to lead. Yet, this transitional vision stage for the emerging leader is crucial because he or she understands God's clarifying, sharpening, and personalizing work in his or her own life.

In *Phase Three*, the emerging leader becomes an influential leader in their own right. They have identified the vision, values, spiritual gifts, self-awareness, skills and strategies God has uniquely given them. The leader now operates out of a clear sense of vision and destiny. Under the sharpening leadership of the Holy Spirit, they have discovered their own personal ministry philosophy...and they begin to attract emerging leaders. The leadership cycle continues. Clinton wisely counsels, *"Don't assume someone else's ministry philosophy. Let God show you yours."*[2]

One of the useful ways we can help leaders distinguish the seasons of their journey comes from a process I learned as a missionary with CRM (Church Resource Ministries). I'm grateful to my friend Dr. Terry Walling for introducing me to it. It's normally known simply as the "Personal Timeline." It can been done in two stages:

First, the Symbol Time-Line Exercise. Recreate on paper your life journey up to this point using symbols and key words. It's especially meaningful and fun for more artistic folks and somewhat uncomfortable for those who aren't, but it allows you to use your right brain expressively. People are often surprised at what they create as they tell their story using the symbols.

Next, the Post-it Note© exercise that helps the leader identify God's shaping work in character insights, ministry insights and unique experiences. As leaders write out symbolically their journey (a good right-brain exercise), the CRM materials ask us to notice how:
1. God used key people, circumstances and events to impact

your development (process items).

2. Your life has gone through various phases or seasons of growth and development (development phases).

3. Your life experiences, both positive and negative, have launched you into a great level of growth and ministry (many of these experiences help you develop your life ministry values).[3]

The Post-it© exercise uses different colors to identify key people, places and events (yellow) along with times of pain or crisis (pink) as well as key life lessons (blue) and seasons (green). Here's the process:

1. Capture as many people, places, events and experiences on yellow Post-it© notes, one to a note. Then, put them in chronological order in vertical rows.

2. As you ponder what you see, you'll notice that some of the notes represent times of pain or difficulty. Change those yellow notes to pink. You see some "pink seasons" along your life journey. A major discovery for many people is seeing that major breakthroughs or periods of fruitfulness came right after seasons of suffering if we let God purify, prune and deepen us through them.

3. Step back again and see the bigger picture. What are the major seasons you notice? Capture them in green and put them along the top where they fit.

4. What key life lessons do you see God building into your life? Capture each one on a Post-it© and place them along the bottom of your timeline.

5. Step back again and see the big picture of all the Lord has been doing in your life in growing, humble recognition. Share your Personal Timeline with some trusted friends and ask for their insights. Pray with them about what you see.

Guiding a leader through the Personal Timeline exercise is a great aid as the leader gains greater clarity on his or her values, vision and personal calling statement. Understanding the bigger picture in the context of the season of his or her life is also crucial. In my own journey, the realization of my own seasons and God's shaping has been immensely important.

Coach Yourself Forward

As we described the three phases leaders go through, which phase are you in now?

Do the Symbol timeline exercise...what significant pictures of symbols surfaced?

Do the Post-it© note timeline exercise. Pay special attention to the pink seasons of suffering and what came after. What life lessons is the Lord clarifying for you?

How is the Lord redeeming your suffering?

Worshipping on an Easter Sunday morning with a packed church of passionate fellow believers in St. Petersburg, Russia was an unforgettable experience for me. A Russian worship service is far different from what we often experience in America. They are often two to three hours long, blending several periods of congregational singing, poems, prayer, offerings, children's choirs and at least three sermons. As a guest pastor from an American church that had supported this church for several years, they invited me to be one of the preachers that day. One of the men who spoke before me was an older man. From the moment he stood behind the pulpit to preach, I was captivated by him. I could only understand what he was saying through a whispering translator, but oh, what his face communicated needed no words! He literally glowed as he spoke about Jesus, his face shining with joy. It was a glow I had rarely seen before...and rarely seen since. Later I found he was the father of my host. He explained that his father had spent a long time imprisoned in the harsh, brutal segregation of Russian confinement because of his faithful commitment to Jesus. In his suffering, my friend's father experienced a depth of intimacy and intensity in his relationship with Jesus that comes from knowing that Jesus is literally all you have. In an environment where the line between life and death is very thin and fragile, Jesus becomes Life Himself. I learned from that incredible man of God that there is a radiance that only comes from going through the valley of the shadow of death with Jesus.

Out of agonizing, deep, redeemed suffering can come an attractive, divinely radiant life.

-Tim Roehl

Few of us have or will suffer like that man, but all of us have suffered, many of us deeply. What we choose to do with that suffering influences whether we are hurt or healed, bitter or better...someone who bruises others or blesses others.

As was mentioned before, at the heart of all these is the leader's own understanding of who God is in their life and what He is trying to accomplish through circumstances. Dallas Willard notes, "We will never have the easy, unhesitating love of God that makes obedience to Jesus our natural response unless we are absolutely sure that *it is good for us to be and to be who we are*. This means we must have no doubt that the path appointed for us—when and where and to whom we were born is good and that nothing irredeemable has happened to us or can happen to us on our way to our destiny in God's full world...*it is confidence in the invariably overriding intention of God for our good*, with respect to all the evil and suffering that may befall us on life's journey, that secures us in peace and joy. We must be sure of that intention if we are to be free and able, like Joseph, to simply do what we know to be right." [emphasis added][9]

Terry Walling describes suffering in some helpful ways, which he depicts as "negative preparation" in the leadership journey. He identifies process items to help leaders better understand their critical incidents in their development. Some deal with God's ongoing, recurring processing throughout life. Others deal with more situational conflict or negative processing. Walling gives some portrayals of suffering in this context. Suffering comes to every life. How a leader handles suffering in its various forms is especially crucial to the shaping of their character and leadership capacity. If you are coaching someone through their suffering, the ability to help them see a bigger picture and process pain is vital. Our ability to listen compassionately is a primary coaching skill at this point. Our ability to ask wise questions and help the leader think through what God is doing is also essential. Our ability to pray for and with leaders in pain is of great worth in the shaping and healing God is doing through suffering.

Process Items in Leadership Preparation[10]

Suffering Process Item	Definition	Examples
Negative Preparation	Specific experiences or conflicts that focus and free leaders for their next stage of development.	Character challenge, ministry crisis, grass-is-greener" syndrome.
Life Crisis	Intense situations of pressure that test and teach dependence.	Health, finances, personality friction, church splits, ministry attack.
Ministry Conflict	Ministry conflicts God uses to help shape ministry philosophy and values.	People struggles, organizational restructuring, facing change.
Leadership Backlash	Ramifications occur because of a decision made by a leader.	Learning perseverance, clarifying vision, wounds, relational conflicts, faith challenges.
Isolation	God sets aside a leader from normal ministry involvement to hear from Him in a deeper way.	Sickness, education, self-renewal, ending of ministry, termination.

Review our "Suffering as Preparation" chart. What personal experiences come to mind? How did you respond to them? I've found to my chagrin that if I missed the lessons God had for me in suffering, He was gracious enough to let me go through them again so I could learn what He had in mind the first time! I've learned to pray, "Lord, please let me squeeze every drop of learning and growth from this suffering so I honor You...and so I don't have to go through this again!"

Only an All-Knowing Wise Savior can redeem our suffering so that it makes us more like Him and draws others to Him. Knowing that can allow us to say as Joseph did in Genesis 50:19-20:

> *"But Joseph said to them, 'Don't be afraid. Am I in the place of God? You intended to harm me, but God intended it for good to accomplish what is now being done, the saving of many lives."* (NIV)

Earlier in this chapter we looked briefly at the importance and a process for forgiving. If the Lord is speaking to you about living in the freedom of forgiveness, make those choices.

How do you cooperate with God in redeeming suffering? The Lord does the healing, we do the yielding.

Going through a season of suffering, the Lord invited me to pray in these ways...

Lord, I repent for what I'm responsible for.
If part of your suffering is self-inflicted, face it honestly and ask the Lord to set you on a different path. In its simplest form, repenting affects our head, our heart and our hands. Repenting brings a changed mind about the wrong direction that led to the bad decisions, a changed heart that now wants to go God's direction and a changed lifestyle that represents ongoing decisions with a new devotion in a new direction. Repenting releases a redirected peace and joy from Jesus.

Lord, redeem this suffering.
Claim the healing that is ours because of Jesus' suffering on the Cross... *"by His stripes we are healed and made whole."* (Isaiah 53:5, KJV, TEV) Lord, please leverage my suffering so I can help others who are suffering in similar ways.

"Praise be to the God and Father of our Lord Jesus Christ, the Father of compassion and the God of all comfort, who comforts us in all our troubles, so that we can comfort those in any trouble with the comfort we ourselves receive from God. For just as we share abundantly in the sufferings of Christ, so also our comfort abounds through Christ." (II Corinthians 1:3-5, NIV)

Lord, reconcile relationships.
Believe that He can reconcile relationships that appear beyond repair. Follow His leading with wisdom and courage beyond your feelings. Do what you can and let God do what only He can do.

Lord, restore what's been lost.
The Lord can *"restore the years the locusts have eaten."* (Joel 2:25 KJV)

Lord, reign in all this!
Declare *"Your Kingdom come, Your will be done on earth as it is in heaven..."* (Matthew 6:10 NIV)

You already know that this isn't instant or easy...but God can and will redeem the suffering in your life even to the point that He can use the hard things that happened to you to help and heal others with His love.

Coach Yourself Forward

What did you learn in this section about how God redeems suffering?

What suffering needs healing in your life?

What are you going to do about it?

Who can help you on the healing journey?

Desert

Not long ago I was in the Arizona desert.

I'm not accustomed to its conditions, so my initial reaction going in was one of shock.

It was barren. There was far more colorless sand and rocks covering the ground than anything green with life. There was little shade, little growth, little life...little anything but stark barrenness. There were few landmarks to gain perspective by. I knew it could be very easy to get lost in the desert.

It was unstable. The sand in most places was deep, easily coming up to my ankles, over the side of my shoes, getting into my shoes and filling them with gritty irritation. Walking was three times harder than on solid ground. Progress was slower. Each step was a drain on my strength. It is hard to move quickly when every step is on ground that shifts beneath you as you walk.

It was hot. The sun reflected off the sand and intensified its searing effects. Exposed skin burning from the combination of sun and sand came quickly. Many of the rocks I saw were black...burnt, cracked and broken from the overwhelming effect of the heat that beat down on them day after cloudless day. It appeared as if the cumulative effect of the heat was literally shriveling solid stone.

It was unsettling. The landscape was marked by deep ravines slashed through the sand by infrequent but devastating downpours. The rain didn't come often, but when it did, if a person wasn't on high ground the flash flood could have lethal implications. Rain was longed for and feared at the same time.

I also knew that beneath some of those rocks and ledges dangerous creatures lurked. Fangs, tails and stingers were only a thoughtless step or reach away. I had to be conscious and careful as I slogged through the sand, scaled the arroyos and climbed around on the rocks.

I decided I did not like the desert.

Yet, since I was there and at the mercy of someone else to transport me out, I was forced to take a closer look at this current desert exposure. I was increasingly surprised by what I saw.

There was life among the barrenness. Barrel cactus, ocotillo, palos verde and tiny flowers were blooming all around me. The meager amount of rain had been stored up in those plants' roots in the depths of the sand. Brilliant, beautiful, varied colors were all around me. The vibrant colors of the flowers were only accentuated by the barren background. I could find beauty even in the midst of barrenness There was stability in the midst of the shifting sands. If I looked ahead and walked with careful purpose, there were indeed trails on solid ground. Others had been in this desert before me. They had found a way to walk with more stability than I had thought possible. I could, in my naive thinking, blaze a new trail...and walk the hard way. Or...I could look for the old paths others had walked before and learn from their wisdom. In the desert I learned to look for the wisdom of those who had walked that way before.

It was hot. There wasn't a lot I could do about changing the temperature...but there were ways to adapt to it. I couldn't change the heat...but I could learn how to live in it while I was in the desert. There were places to find comforting, cooling shade. I learned sometimes it's better to rest and wait when the heat is at its worst and travel in the cool of the early morning or evening dusk.

Some things about the desert will not change. It's up to us to adapt...or suffer the searing consequences.

There was more safety than I had expected. Yes, rattlers, tarantulas and scorpions do inhabit the desert. Yes, they are dangerous and poisonous. Yet, as I came to understand where I might encounter them and how I could deal with them, the fear that had first gripped and almost paralyzed me subsided. Still, I knew that I could never become over confident. Alert caution is still the better part of valor when you are in the desert.

I decided the desert wasn't so bad after all. I wouldn't want to live there, but if by necessity I had to go into the desert I knew that I could find beauty, wisdom from those who had walked before me, and the ability to learn and grow there. The desert ultimately helped shape me into a better man.

Lord, the deserts in my seasons of the soul aren't really any different from the deserts of Arizona, are they?

-Tim Roehl

4

Look In

Know Yourself from the Inside Out

Eagle
(Isaiah 40:28-31; I Samuel 16:7; I Corinthians 12:11,18)

I saw an eagle today.

It was the first time I'd had the privilege of seeing one in the wild...where God had created it to rule its domain.

It was sitting on the branch of a tall dead tree where it was able to visually survey its territory, raising the status of the tree from useless deadwood to a regal throne.

Actually, at first I was a bit surprised. The bird was quite comfortable on its perch, patiently waiting for its cue to take wing, but it wasn't as beautiful close up as I thought it would be. It was almost scruffy, with its feathers looking as windblown as my hair did after being out in the boat all day. I must confess that in spite of the thrill of seeing our national symbol close up for the first time, I was almost disappointed.

Then the eagle took wing....and suddenly my thrill increased tenfold! It unfurled its wings and seemed to fill the sky with its feathery span. Two quick, powerful beats of those wings....and then it caught an updraft! Wings spread, it effortlessly began to soar higher and higher, riding the wind currents in an ever-widening circle. It was a majestic, beautiful sight, one that kept my eyes locked onto the bird until the eagle was out of my sight. I was seeing that eagle in its element the way God had intended....riding an updraft toward heaven. It was awesome.

Then I realized something very important. At first, close up, sitting on a perch, the bird had not impressed me like I thought it would. It was when it was in the sky, sun glistening off its beautiful white head and tail, that the eagle seemed to grow in stature. That eagle was meant to soar, not sit. It was as if it flew with a sense of its Creator's joy when it rode the wind. When I realized that, my respect, thrill and awe at the sight of such a regal member of God's creation grew as well. My first impression was short sighted and shallow. I vowed not to make that mistake with the eagle again.

I've made the same mistake with people.

I've watched men who at first meeting were not impressive in physical appearance or social presence. Yet, I've also watched some of those men stand behind a pulpit to proclaim God's Word in the power of God's Spirit....and it seemed that they grew to be ten feet tall. I was seeing them then from a supernatural viewpoint. They were doing what God has created them in His infinite wisdom to do....and that made all the difference. It was in that setting that they "spread their wings" and caught God's updraft, riding the wind of His sufficiency and feeling His pleasure in fulfilling His plan for their lives.

The outward appearance matters little when there is the heart of an eagle within.

I've had the same feeling in other settings....
A doctor applying his healing touch to a hurting patient.
A salesman whose eyes light up as he describes the
   product he knows inside out.
   A father showing his sons how to catch fish or build
   with wood.
   A mother rocking her small child to sleep late
   at night.

A coach energizing his team with wisdom in the
final minute of the game.
A teacher making Jesus come alive to the hearts
of small children.

In their special realm, their labor of love had a divine
quality far above the ordinary.

Why? Because God has created every person with a
purpose...a purpose so majestic and regal that it parallels
that of the eagle I saw soaring.

When we find His place for us and begin to fulfill His
purpose with the updraft of His power, we become an
eagle in our own setting.

We're not made to perch on the deadwood of our own
strength.

We're made to fly! We're made to soar with our wings
spread, riding the wind of God's Spirit, feeling His
pleasure as we go higher and higher in the realm and
the purpose He created us to fulfill, living for eternity
and bringing glory to our Savior.

Life was meant to be lived in the supernatural with an
eagle heart. God wants us to soar on the heights with
Him, enjoying His updraft from heaven in all we do.
When we take wing as an eagle, life becomes supernatural.
Anything else is shabby and shallow. Yet, God leaves the
choice to every person...to perch limited to our own
power on deadwood, earthbound...or soar without limit
with Him, heaven bound.

Lord, I choose to be an eagle...
and I choose to see the eagle in others, too.

--Tim Roehl at Lake of the Woods

How do you "see" yourself?

> *"Love the Lord your God with all your heart, soul, mind and strength...and your neighbor as yourself." (Mark 12:30,31 NIV)*

> *"Oh, yes, You shaped me first inside, then out...I thank You, High God—You're breathtaking! Body and soul, I am marvelously made...You know me inside and out." (Psalm 139:13,14,15 The Message)*

> *"In view of God's mercy...be transformed...by the grace given me...make an honest evaluation of yourself...we who are many are one Body in Christ...we are members of one another... according to the grace given us, we have different gifts... overcome evil with good." (Romans 12:1-6,21)*

> *"By the grace of God, I am who I am...and His grace to me is not wasted...and I won't waste it! It is fruitful and effective... it fuels all I do..." (I Corinthians 15;10, Tim Roehl)*

As we gain a true view of Who God is, we can also receive a true view of who we are.

If we have a true view of the Lord, we see ourselves as...
 His highest creation, made in His image,
  His greatest joy,
   of infinite value,
    of such worth that the Father would send Jesus to redeem
     us and restore our broken, separated relationship with Him.

We are the beloved sons and daughters of the King of the Universe!

The Holy Spirit fills us, thrills us, keeps us clean with holy love, guides us with truth, empowers us to live His best, gives us His grace gifts to bless others, continually reminds us that He chose us in adopting love.

He takes great delight in us.

His posture is always inviting us to intimacy with Him.

We can live an abundant, fulfilling, overcoming, life of righteousness, peace and joy in Him!

Our identity is grounded in grace and fueled by holy love.

Even when we fail, He invites us to come back home to Him.

That's a true view of who we are in Him!

But, if we have a false view of God, we see ourselves as...
  ongoing objects of God's wrath,
    never measuring up to His impossible standards,
      always failing Him
        living in a cycle of failure, frustration and continually
          begging for forgiveness.

We are slaves of a distant, demanding Sovereign Ruler who uses us only for His own ends. His posture is shaking His finger at us, demanding that we try harder, yet always disappointed with our efforts.

The best we can hope for is an ongoing cycle of failure, self-effort and pleas for mercy.

That's a false view of who we are.

Here are some foundational issues to help us get a true view of how we are meant to see ourselves...

Every person is...

Created in the *image* of God. (Psalm 139:14) *"...I am fearfully and wonderfully made..."* This is the foundation and common ground for *every* person. Our purpose and identity, security and significance begin here...our destiny is to be restored to that relationship and image!

Instilled with baseline personality...God-given and unique natural wiring, which includes underlying motivation, usual and effective style, underlying needs, stress behavior, how we process information, solve problems and relate to others.

Influenced by...
  Culture and home country
  Family of origin
  Past experiences
  Current environment and circumstances
  Relational dynamics
  Physical, mental/emotional and spiritual condition

Life in Jesus gives us...

A life *infused* with holy love, able to respond like Jesus through our personality because of the ongoing purifying and maturing work on the Holy Spirit.

Supernatural spiritual gifts--God's power *imparted* above and beyond our personality!

Opportunity for *intentional*, integrated, authentic biblical community and redemptive ministry as His Body and Team... we all are a part of His great redemptive mission in our world!

We are both a natural being created in the image of God AND a supernatural being sharing the life of God!

When I was in college, I learned something that has been foundational for me ever since. I learned that if we have our identity in something other than Jesus, such as...

A particular doctrinal persuasion (Calvinist, Wesleyan, Charismatic, Lutheran, Catholic, etc.)

Personal achievement (what I can do for God...or for myself)
Self-effort (working harder to be more spiritual)
Positional power or influence
Possessions...

...we're never really secure. When I compare myself to others I wind up being critical with my need to be "right." I never know if I've achieved enough, worked hard enough, acquired enough or climbed high enough on the right ladder. I saw a lot of people struggling because of those issues.

Then I saw others (not nearly enough) whose identity and security was in Jesus. They didn't have to compare or strive or criticize... they could walk among and work with all kinds of people with a non-anxious presence, even those who were very different than them. The difference was Jesus as the center of a grace-based identity.

I chose to be a Jesus guy. That's made all the difference.

Coach Yourself Forward

How do you see yourself?

What is God saying to you right now about who you are to Him?

What lies do you need to reject?

What truths do you need to receive?

How would you describe yourself? Write out a description of who you are based on a true view of God and a true view of yourself.

My Identity...In Christ

I Am Accepted!

John 1:12	*I am God's child.*
John 15:15	*I am Christ's friend.*
Romans 5:1	*I have been justified...made right with God.*
I Corinthians. 6:17	*I am united with the Lord, one in Spirit with Him.*
I Corinthians 6:19,20	*I have been bought with a price...I belong to God.*
I Corinthians. 12:27	*I am a member of Christ's Body.*
II Corinthians 5:17	*I am a new creation...a brand new person inside!*
I John 1:9	*I am forgiven and cleansed from my sins.*

I Am Secure!

Romans 8:1,2	*I am free from condemnation.*
Romans 8:28	*I am assured God will work all things together for good.*
Romans 8:31ff	*I am free from any condemning charges against me.*
Romans 8:35ff	*Nothing can separate me from God's love.*
II Corinthians 1:20-22	*I am established, anointed and sealed by God.*
Colossians 3:3	*I am hidden with Christ in God.*
Philippians 1:6	*God will complete the good work He has started in me!*
Philippians 3:20	*I am a citizen of heaven.*
II Timothy 1:7	*God has given me power, love and a sound mind, not fear.*
Hebrews 4:16	*God will give me grace and mercy in time of need.*
I John 5:18	*I am born of God...the evil one can't touch me.*

I Am Significant!

Matthew 5:13,14 I am the salt and light of the earth.
John 15:1, 5   I am a branch of the True Vine, a channel of His life.
John 15:16   Jesus has chosen me to bear much fruit for Him.
Acts 1:8   I am a witness for Christ.
I Corinthians 3:16 I am God's Temple.
II Corinthians 6:1 I am God's co-worker.
Ephesians 2:6   I am seated with Christ in heavenly realms.
Ephesians 2:10   I am God's workmanship, created for good works.
Ephesians 3:12   I may approach God with freedom and confidence.
Philippians 4:13 I can do all things through Christ Who gives me strength.

(Adapted from Neil Anderson)

What's Your Natural Wiring?

Personality. Temperament. Natural wiring. No matter what words you use, it's essential that you have good awareness of this aspect of how the Lord made you. When we look at our natural wiring, we grow in our understanding of our tendencies and behaviors. For example, consider:

What energizes, fuels and nourishes you
What drains and depletes you
What motivates you
How you work when you are most effective
The support or environment you need to be effective
How you process information
How you approach solving problems
Your communication style
How you behave when you are stressed
Where you may be vulnerable
How you best contribute on a team
Who you need with you on a team
Whether you are more task oriented or people oriented
Whether you are more of a big picture person or more
    detail-oriented
Your expectations of how you want others to treat you

"You can tell all that from knowing your natural wiring?!" you may ask. We can get over 80% of the picture of ourselves through knowing your personality patterns. There are plenty of influences that affect us, such as our home culture, the environment we grew up in and the impact of defining life experiences, as we talked about earlier. However, our baseline personality is pretty much hard wired into us...hence, we call it natural wiring.

"How can I learn more about my natural wiring?"

There are many inventories available that give you different ways to learn more about your personality patterns. However, many people are hesitant to take some kind of "test" out of concerns that they might be pigeon-holed, put in a box or the results might be held against you. Personality profiles are never to be used to harm people! Any profile or inventory you take should be only a part of a discovery and discernment process to understand how God made you...both in your natural wiring and your supernatural gifting.

A Profile/Process is NOT...	A Profile/Process IS...
1. A way to put you in a box or pigeon hole you	1. A way to help you see and steward who you are
2. An excuse for unhealthy or sinful behavior	2. A way to help you express needs in a healthy way
3. A test you pass or fail	3. A way to stimulate conversation and discovery
4. The last word on your identity	4. Dependent on the Spirit's guidance and grace
5. Only about you	5. About you, your team and Kingdom ministry

Think about these principles in a self-discovery process:

When we consider the different personality inventories you may utilize, the one I like for ease of understanding and simplicity is the DISC Profile. You can find in many forms both in print and online. However, the profile I like most for its depth and comprehensiveness is the Birkman Method. (www.birkman.com) The Birkman Method has been taken by over fifty million people over the past 50 years and is available in over twenty languages. It is used extensively in business and academics. The Birkman profile helps you "see" things that no other profile and process has, especially assisting you understand the things others can't see (underlying motivation and underlying needs). In fact, the list I made above are all things the Birkman profile helps you identify and apply.

Remember, every personality style has strengths and weaknesses. God wired us for a purpose...on purpose! When His grace begins to redeem, heal and cleanse what sin and life's wounds have done to us, we are free to be who He created us to be...to live our true personality and patterns in healthy, gracious ways! Remember this all important reality: the Difference Maker in all things is the purifying and maturing work of the Holy Spirit in our lives! No matter what your personality, God's goal for us is character that responds as Jesus would in all situations. Character matters most.

"By the grace of God, I am who I am...and His grace to me is not wasted...and I won't waste it! It is fruitful and effective...it fuels all I do..." (I Corinthians 15:10, Tim Roehl)

Coach Yourself Forward

Go back to our list of tendencies and behaviors. Do your own "first pass" at describing them? What did you learn?

Have someone who knows you and loves you do the same thing with that list. What did they "see" that surprises or affirms you?

If you haven't done a more formal, intentional personality profile, plan to do one. My recommendation is to blend your personality and spiritual gifts as offered by the Grip-Birkman profile. Go to www.gripbirkman.com to learn more.

What are Your Spiritual Gifts?

> In the first church we pastored, a missionary friend of
> ours came to minister. Gordon is a gracious, gentle man
> who doesn't call attention to himself. He would not
> describe himself as extroverted or dynamic. I asked
> Gordon if he'd like to preach in our morning service. He
> agreed with a quiet smile.
>
> I sat behind Gordon as he got up to speak. As he began
> to preach, Gordon grew ten feet tall right before my
> eyes! He spoke with power and authority far beyond his
> personality. I was watching Gordon's gift of teaching
> supernaturally at work. When I see that happen in
> others now, I call it the "ten foot tall principle." God's
> power supernaturally through His gifts extends us
> beyond ourselves. We become "ten feet tall" in the Spirit!

If you have been born into God's family and enjoying life as His
child, one of the wonderful benefits is receiving spiritual gifts from
the Holy Spirit. We are not only natural beings, we are also supernatural! When we talk about spiritual gifts, there is a broad range
of perspectives across the Body of Christ. On one side of the spectrum, some would say that there are no such things as spiritual
gifts in our day... that all ended when the first generation apostles
died. On the other side of the spectrum, some would say that you
have to have a particular spiritual gift (usually the gift of tongues)
to even be a Christian. Some acknowledge certain spiritual gifts,
but not others. Some list nine gifts...some more than twenty!

For our purposes, we are going to look at spiritual gifts as God's
power given by the Holy Spirit in special ways above and beyond
our personality so we can bless and benefit others. Spiritual gifts
are not just an extension of our personality. They are often quite
different...so different from our natural wiring that when they are
operating through a clean heart fueled by holy love all we can do is
say in wonder, "That had to be God!"

Also, consider these principles when you think about spiritual gifts:

- Focus on the Giver more than His gifts.
- The greatest evidence of being filled with the Spirit is love from a pure heart. (I Corinthians 12:31-13:13, I Timothy 1:5)
- The fruit of the Spirit (Galatians 5:22,23) is needed to balance and maximize the power of the gifts.

You may ask, "How can I come to understand and exercise the spiritual gifts God's given me?" What's the difference between natural ability and God-given spiritual gifts? Great question. My friend Dr. Paul Ford taught me a question that helps to differentiate between the two. Ask yourself, *"When do I most often experience God's power, joy and fruit?"* You might be very good at a particular skill, but if you can't honestly say that you experience God's power, joy and fruit when you do it, it is most likely natural ability. On the other hand, when you find yourself humbled and amazed at what happens when you do something and the results are beyond what your natural ability, it is probably a spiritual gift. Even if a person has never taken a spiritual gifts inventory, answering that question often gives us indicators about our spiritual gifts.

As with personality profiles, there are many spiritual gifts inventories you can take. However, most of them just give you a score that indicates what your gifts might be. The spiritual gifts profiles that I feel are most helpful are both authored by my friend and ministry team mate Dr. Paul Ford. Paul and I served on a team together as missionaries with Church Resource Ministries (CRM) and have ministered together in many nations and cultures. Paul's approach to understanding spiritual gifts in the context of stewarding our relationships and God's power is wise and biblical. *Discovering Your Ministry Identity (DYMI)* and *Your Leadership Grip (YLG)* are very similar. They can both be taken in a paper version. You can also take *Your Leadership Grip* online by going to www.leadershipgrip.com.

What makes these spiritual gift profiles so powerful is how they allow us to see our gifts from three different angles. These three questions give focus to understanding our gifts:

Where are you powerful?
Where are you weak?
Who do you need?

As we look at those three angles, we are able to get more clarity on those questions...

The first angle is your gift mix...your "supernatural me." This is not so much a list of your gifts as much as a mix of your gifts. They complement and coordinate God's power in and through you. Equipping gifts are more verbal in nature—God's power shows up most through your words. Examples of equipping gifts include: *pastor, leadership, evangelism, teaching, wisdom, exhortation, faith.* Some would include *prophecy, missionary and knowledge.* Some faith traditions include gifts like *miracles, healing, tongues, and interpretation.*

Supporting gifts are when God's power shows up through your actions. Examples of supporting gifts include: *helps, service, mercy, administration and giving.* Some would add gifts like *poverty or celibacy.* Sometimes we have all equipping gifts, sometimes all supporting gifts, sometimes a combination of both.

The second angle is your team styles...your "supernatural we." This is how your spiritual gifts operate in a team setting. DYMI and YLG team styles are "Let's Go," "Let Me Help You," "Let's Stay Together" and "Let's Be Careful." We identify your strongest team styles and what team style you need. We also learn more how whether God's power shows up when you are "up front," "alongside" or both. Acknowledging our needs reminds us that we have "divinely designed weakness"—we need each other in the Body of Christ!

The third angle is your body building roles...your "supernatural they." This is how God stewards your gifts to accomplish His Kingdom purposes...the Great Commission side of your gifts. Body Building Roles in DYMI and YLG include: "Vision Sharer," "Active Listener," "Values Keeper," "Team Builder," "Supporting

Releaser" and "Equipping Releaser." Again, we identify your strongest body building roles and who you need to better fulfill the Great Commission.

Here's what the gifts triangle looks like:

As we discover God's power from these three perspectives, it brings us the best to describe how we most often experience God's power, joy and fruit. *Your Leadership Grip* and *Discovering Your Ministry Identity* are especially affirming for those with supporting gifts and alongside power. Too many Christians live with the false idea that the only truly gifted people are the ones who can stand up front and speak well. That's not true! In God's family, all His children are significant because of the Cross! All His children have a role to play in His great redemptive work and gifts to play their part with His power and grace. We all steward His power so His message of salvation through Jesus can come to others. We all need each other. He gets all the glory!

Bring the natural and supernatural together...

Can you bring the natural side of who you are and the super-natural side together to see yourself in both ways? Yes! Dr. Paul Ford pioneered a process that brings together the power of the Birkman Method and his spiritual gifts profiles. We call it the Grip Birkman process. You can learn more about how to take the profiles and profit from the insights they provide at www.gripbirkman.com. There are hundreds of Grip Birkman coaches who can help you get the maximum benefit of the Grip Birkman profile. The Grip Birkman process is very affirming and useful for individuals, teams, couples and ministries. Many churches, mission agencies, universities and denominations use the Grip Birkman as a vital part of their ministry profiling and placement process.

One more aspect of the Grip Birkman process takes you beyond the scores on an inventory to much more discovery and clarity. We call it the *"Four Passes of Honest Evaluation"* based on Romans 12:3:

> *"For by the grace given me I say to every one of you: Do not think of yourself more highly than you ought, but rather think of yourself with sober judgment (an honest evaluation of yourself), in accordance with the measure of faith God has given you." (Romans 12:3)*

In order to make an honest evaluation and get the best picture of who you are, you can use these "four passes":

1. *Review the report*...let the report speak to you from its perspective.
2. *Reflect on your experiences*...what does this look like in your life? Personalize what's on paper.
3. *Receive(d) feedback*...what have others said *to* you or *about* you that gives us more insights?
4. *Respond to the Spirit*...what is the Lord saying? What actions does He want you to take?

You can use these "Four Passes of Honest Evaluation" in many ways. It's a great coaching resource.

Coach Yourself Forward

Check out the Grip Birkman process... you'll be glad you did!

When do you feel "ten feet tall" in the Spirit's power?

How well do you know and use your spiritual gifts?

What's holding you back?

When you consider the wonder of being a child of God and the unique ways He has wired and gifted you, it is humbling and amazing! Psalm 139 uses the words "fearful and wonderful." He made us for specific, eternal purposes...to fit and flourish! Yet, when we look at ourselves, sometimes we feel wonderful and sometimes fearful!

Too many hold back from stepping into the fit and flourish life Jesus wants for them. With all the supernatural grace and heavenly resources available for us, what could hold us back?

Earlier we highlighted how important it is to realize how we "see" God and "see" ourselves. Revisit those issues...how might they be holding you back?

At One Mission Society, we do an exercise during our One Weekend experience we call the "Berry Bush" (as in "Barriers"). We help people identify the more obvious barriers that are holding them back in the form of our "berries"—the fruit of our fears. However, all the "fruit" grows from a "root." Each berry/barrier finds its source rooted in a lie about God's nature. We have each person identify their berries/barriers and then trace them back to their roots. For example, a common berry/barrier is a fear of raising the support needed to go to a mission field. The root often is "God can't be trusted to provide." You get the idea.

Then we go a step further by equipping ourselves to deal with the berries/barriers at the root level. How do you demolish a lie? How do you deal with a poisonous berry bush? Do you pick off the berries? No... you pull it out at the root!

Replace your berry bush with a Truth Tree. Declare and embrace the truth! For each lie we may believe that holds us back, our Promise Maker has dozens of promises from His eternally true Promise Book to claim and receive. Remember, the Promise Maker is also the Promise Keeper!

Coach Yourself Forward

Take some time right now and do your own Berry Bush and Truth Tree:

My Berry Bush

Roots/Lies   **Berries/Barriers**

My Truth Tree

Truth Roots   **Promise Fruits**

How will you keep planting and nourishing your truth roots?

How will you guard against and cut out root lies?

Who will help you?

Who can you help?

5
Look At
Clarify Your Why, How, Who

*"Great leaders love people and use things to do Kingdom ministry.
Other leaders love things and use people to build their empire."*

*"God calls us as Kingdom leaders
to be led more BY Jesus,
Knowing Him and understanding His will,
To lead more LIKE Jesus,
Enabling His people to be a reconciling community,
To lead more TO Jesus
Serving His redemptive purposes in our generation."
(Dr. Leighton Ford's Vision Statement
for the Arrow Leadership Program)*

Recipe for a Giant of God

Start with the raw material of an acute hunger for God
and a humble, teachable spirit that longs to become
like Jesus and lead others to Jesus.

Mix in massive amounts of worship and the Word
seasoned with prayer.

Add the yeast of people—parents, a mate, heroes,
friends, mentors, giants of the past, teachers, children,
heart-holders, encouragers, kindred spirits, teammates, enemies and those who come to us as unexpected
appointments by God. There is no such thing as a
self-made giant.

Watch closely to see if there is a growing sense of destiny.

Stir in cups of suffering, solitude, spiritual gifts and servanthood. Each recipe calls for amounts unique to each emerging giant of God.

Sprinkle in liberal amounts of joy from the Holy Spirit and a healthy sense of humor. Remember, no one likes a stuffy giant!

Allow time for the mixture to process. When you see it begin to bubble with passion, roll out the mixture on the formative board of daily living. Apply the sharp knife of discipline around the pattern of God's vision for that giant. Begin to trim the giant to take his or her final God-ordained shape.

Allow more time for the passion and vision to mature. Take the mixture and stretch it at its heart until it seems to reach the breaking point, let it rest in the love of God, then stretch it some more. The giant needs to be broad, but also deep. If the mixture looks like it is still too thin, ask the Holy Spirit if He wants to blend in more of the previous ingredients. Season the mixture with even more prayer. We dare not allow our giant to come out shallow and half-baked. We need a giant to be as deep and pure as he is tall and fruitful.

Along the way, let others taste the recipe. See if they enjoy it and want to get a copy for themselves. If you see others being influenced by this emerging giant, you'll know your giant is developing according to God's plan.

Your giant will grow to be very visible on the spiritual landscape of life, yet always appear to be approachable to others. The recipe is meant to feed multitudes...one at a time.

Your giant will never quite be a finished product, but as time goes on you will notice that your giant is finishing well.

You will see evidence that all the ingredients are blended just as the Lord intended.

As others come to Christ because of the giant and you notice how much the giant conforms to the image of Christ, step back in wonder.

Glorify our Giant God—for surely this giant of God can only be a miracle of His!

—Tim Roehl, based on talks by Dr. Leighton Ford and Dr. Paul Stanley

What's Your Motivation?

Books, articles, podcasts, workshops, models, styles, examples, theories and definitions abound about leadership. I've adopted a very simple definition from Dr. John Maxwell, a leadership hero of mine. Dr. Maxwell says, "Leadership is influence." In that sense, everyone is a leader because everyone has influence to some degree. Our leadership styles and scope are influenced a lot by our personality, opportunity and God's sovereign blessing.

What motivates our leadership, however, is a heart issue.

As I've thought about leadership and watched leaders, three main leadership types come to the forefront.

Transactional leadership uses people to accomplish a leader's ends. Sometimes it is as simple as being hired to do a job and the leader treats people with respect and pays a fair wage. That type of transactional leadership can be appropriate if both parties treat each other with mutual respect. Other times, however, transactional leadership springs from an unhealthy source. People being used by a transactional leader get a much different sense of their value to them: "You are a means to my end....I'm the leader, you're the follower...I'm the boss, you're the employee...I tell you what to do, you do it...I will use you to accomplish my purposes, and when I'm done with you, don't expect anything from me." This type of leader wants to build their own empire. Although their language may sound spiritual, their motives all come back to self.

Transformational leadership is often considered the highest type of leadership in most leadership thinking. A transformational leader is able to call others to a compelling vision and rally them to accomplish something great. Many people want to be inspired to a cause greater than themselves. God created us for greatness! A leader with the personality to influence a large number of people and organizational skills to bring a team together can accomplish great things. Transformational leaders sometimes add value and show honor to their followers, sometimes not. I've seen some leaders who are very gifted and focused to the point of only being able to see things from their point of view or with their own vision in mind. Focused leaders have great strengths but also some glaring weaknesses. If it's not going to benefit them, they won't invest time, energy or other resources on behalf on someone else.

There is one more type of leadership I've found that transcends all others. Jesus is our Ultimate Leader, the One who perfectly blends sovereign authority with servant ability. He's the One who made the ultimate sacrificial transaction on our behalf when He paid a debt we could never repay to restore our relationship with the Father. He's the One whose motivation was selfless love and whose mission was entirely on behalf of others. I find it in what my friend Steve Ogne and I call "transformissional leadership."

TransforMissional leadership is leadership that has two great purposes in mind for the people they lead. First, transformissional leaders value people and seek to add value to those they lead. They want those they lead to experience the Great Commandment—to love the Lord with all their heart, soul, mind and strength and their neighbors as themselves. (Mark 12:37). They genuinely want God's best for those they lead...a transformed life of holy love.

Second, a transformissional leader helps equip people for their part in the Great Commission. They want to steward their people so they make their maximum Kingdom contribution. We are all called to make disciples wherever we go...we all have a part in God's great redemptive purposes in our world! A transformissional leader has found where they best fit and flourish and helps others do the same...experiencing the fullness of a Great Commandment, Great Commission life.

As I wrote earlier, the Arrow Leadership Program, founded by Leighton Ford, has a beautiful and powerful vision statement for its "Arrow leaders" that beautifully expresses a transformissional view of leadership. I have adopted as an integral part of my own journey since graduating from Arrow: *"God calls us as Kingdom leaders to be led more BY Jesus, knowing Him and understanding His will, to lead more LIKE Jesus, enabling His people to be a reconciling community, to lead more TO Jesus, serving His redemptive purposes in our generation."[11]*

Transformissional leaders are Kingdom leaders. Often in our Arrow journey, we were challenged to be leaders who were committed to build God's kingdom, not our own empires. The major difference between a Kingdom leader and an empire builder is their motivation for ministry. If a leader's motivation is to build his or her own empire, everything he or she does will be stunted and ultimately soured by an undercurrent of selfishness. If the leader's motivation is fueled by a passion for people to come to Christ and God's kingdom reign to be manifested, God's intentions will be fulfilled both for the leader and those they influence. They will finish well and fulfill God's purposes in their generation.

How can we discern ministry motivation and intentionally develop a Kingdom perspective? Here are several insights to consider:

How much "self" is there as you listen to the leader? Does conversation about their dreams, vision, goals, and accomplishments tend to center around themselves and gaining possessions, positions, and power? How much do they talk about others in an honoring way or in a transactional way? To what degree do they desire God's greater Kingdom priorities beyond their own ambition? The issues raised in Matthew 6:19-33 can form a good basis for discussion as you walk with leaders and seek to discern their ministry motivation:

> "Do not lay up for yourselves treasures on earth, where
> moth and rust destroy and where thieves break in and
> steal; but lay up for yourselves treasures in heaven,
> where neither moth nor rust destroys and where thieves
> do not break in and steal. *For where your treasure is,*
> *there your heart will be also.* The lamp of the body is the
> eye. If therefore your eye is good, your whole body will
> be full of light. But if your eye is bad, your whole body
> will be full of darkness. If therefore the light that is in

you is darkness, how great is that darkness! No one can serve two masters; for either he will hate the one and love the other, or else he will be loyal to the one and despise the other. You cannot serve God and mammon. *Therefore I say to you, do not worry about your life, what you will eat or what you will drink; nor about your body, what you will put on.* Is not life more than food and the body more than clothing? Look at the birds of the air, for they neither sow nor reap nor gather into barns; yet your heavenly Father feeds them. Are you not of more value than they? Which of you by worrying can add one cubit to his stature? So why do you worry about clothing? Consider the lilies of the field, how they grow: they neither toil nor spin; and yet I say to you that even Solomon in all his glory was not arrayed like one of these. Now if God so clothes the grass of the field, which today is, and tomorrow is thrown into the oven, will He not much more clothe you, O you of little faith? *Therefore do not worry, saying, "What shall we eat?" or "What shall we drink?" or "What shall we wear"? For after all these things the Gentiles seek. For your heavenly Father knows that you need all these things. But seek first the kingdom of God and His righteousness, and all these things shall be added to you.* (NKJV, emphasis added)

Whether a leader is "seeking first the Kingdom" or not is not easy to discern, for only God knows the heart, but careful and prayerful listening will allow us to raise these issues with the leaders we work with.

What is their sense of "Kingdom team?" A key ministry concept is this: When God sends a leader to an area, He is sending them to join a "team" of leaders whom He is raising up to reach that area. Does the leader you are working with see himself or herself as a part of a bigger team that includes leaders from groups and churches beyond his or her own, or does he or she only see his or her own church and ministry? Does the leader speak well of leaders, churches, and ministries, or does he or she speak negatively in order to make him or herself look better? Has the leader found other "Kingdom teammates" to pray with and for? How willing is the leader to seek fellowship and blessing from others who have been in the area longer and know the ministry history and needs better?

I have a vivid memories of a time when I was a new church planter. Arriving in a new city to plant a church, I felt strongly that the Lord wanted me to find other pastors to pray with...and that I needed to seek their blessing as I "joined the team." As the Lord led me to other pastors in the area, friendships grew and we began to pray together. We became a "band of brothers" from over a half-dozen denominations that prayed, wept, celebrated, ministered together, and formed a Kingdom team for our area. We did strategic intercession drives around our county many times, came together as churches for worship services, and served our ministry area in various ways. Over the course of time we saw as many as five pastors' groups grow up around our area, and over twenty years we continued to pray and reach our area together. The importance of understanding "God's kingdom team" has become an essential part of my coaching as I work with other leaders.

What is the scope of their "harvest vision?" This is a close cousin to "sense of team." When the leader thinks about the harvest, does he or she only think of it in the context and boundaries of their local church? Does the leader "see" only their neighborhood and/or city, or do they see an entire region that needs to be reached for Christ? What is their heart for the whole world? How willing are they to get involved in ministry beyond what will directly benefit their own church ministry? Is the leader's goal to reach as many people for Christ as possible or simply to see their ministry grow even if it is at the expense of other ministries?

One of the key indicators of leaders who are Kingdom-minded versus empire builders is their willingness to invest in ministry that does not directly benefit them. Also, their interest and support for church multiplication and world missions are keys to understanding the scope of their harvest vision.

The significance of Kingdom motivation is all important. It's the difference between purifying or poisoning relationships, between using people or empowering them, between ministry for our Master's glory or building our own significance, between what lasts forever or is limited to our human efforts.

What's *your* motivation for ministry?

Coach Yourself Forward

When we talked about the three types of leadership— transactional, transformational and transformissional—who came to mind? How did you feel as you thought about those people?

Who knows you best and loves you most that will give you honest feedback about what they see about your motivation?

What is the Lord saying to you about your motivation for ministry?

What's Your Ministry Orientation?

"The reason I left you in Crete was that you might straighten out what was left unfinished and appoint elders in every town, as I directed you." (Titus 1:5) This verse reminds us that some are called to plant and initiate, others to develop and coordinate! Paul the pioneer needed the help of Titus the pastor. It's vital to recognize the unique giftings of each ministry orientation!

Ministry orientation is our inclination toward how we approach people and ministry. In its simplest form, our ministry orientation will be along two lines. Some are more pioneering—they like starting new ventures. Others are more pastoring—they like shepherding people.

Here's a way you can compare those two ministry orientations. As you look at the columns, put a check by the words that describe you most. If you feel you are some of both, put a check in the middle. If you lean one way, put the check closer to the terms that fit you best.

Planter/Pioneer	Pastor/Shepherd
- to the "not yet convinced"	- to the already convinced
- likes change/chaos	- likes order
- unpredictable	- predictable
- start	- sustain
- itinerant/regional	- local church
- create, initiate	- nurture, coordinate
- proclamational	- incarnational
- short-term	- long term
- "simple" organization	- increasingly organized and complex
- challenge the status quo	- cherish status quo
- competitive—strive to "win"	- collegial—want to get along

Both styles are important in God's work: we need both types of ministry orientation. However, there is great potential for friction because the priorities will often appear to be at odds. For example, one may value taking risks while the other may value security. Remember, we need each other...honor each other!

Coach Yourself Forward

As you compared the descriptions of ministry orientations, which fits you better?

How well does your ministry involvement fit your ministry orientation? If you were to rate it by percentage (i.e., 50/50, 60/40, 75/25), what does yours look like?

If your ministry orientation is more pioneer-oriented, you might want to go a step further and pray over this list:

Essential Qualities for Spiritual Pioneers

"The best indicator of future performance is past behavior."

1. *Christlike Character*
   - Strong, consistent walk with God. Deep prayer life.
   - Sticks to commitments even under tough circumstances. Perseveres. Bounces back.
   - Strong sense of call
   - Spiritual gifts "package" that includes leadership, faith, discernment, evangelism

2. *Casts Vision*
   - Communicates vision in an inspiring and practical manner.
   - Can "see" into the future with faith
   - Creates and initiates projects from the ground up

3. *Capacity for Excellence*
   - Self-starter and self-managed—strong need to achieve
   - Strong work ethic
   - Strives for authenticity and excellence

4. **Creates Ownership of Ministry**
   - Recruits, coaches and delegates effectively
   - Reproduction mindset—develops an ever widening circle of reproducing leaders and groups
   - Releases others into ministry—assesses gifts, equips wisely
   - Receptive to other's ideas—flexible, yet builds team cohesion and agenda harmony around the vision

5. **Cooperation of Spouse and Family**
   - "Heart agreement" about roles and expectations in ministry
   - Healthy family life
   - Helped by a strong support system of family and friends

6. **Constructive, Compassionate People Skills**
   - Appreciates and accepts a wide variety of people, able to respond with compassion when needs arise
   - Approachable and active in developing relationships
   - Able to handle conflict constructively and deal with difficult people

7. **Consistent Fruitfulness**
   - Consistently develops relationships with unchurched people
   - Continual evidence of people coming to Christ
   - Disciplemaking and church multiplication mindset—sees evangelism as essential.

8. **Community Responsive, Culturally Relevant Ministry Mindset**
   - Studies local community as their mission field—understands the needs and opportunities
   - Starts ministries that meet needs in the community
   - "Seen" in the community as a positive influence
   - Strategic intercession practiced intentionally

(Tim Roehl, adapted from Charles Ridley's *13 Qualities*)

What's your best contribution on a team?

What's the difference between a bowling team and a basketball team?

Think about it...are we all just playing for ourselves and adding up individual scores at the end, or are we indispensable to each other, unable to fully do our part without each other...knowing we all win or lose together?

Fit and flourish living and ministry is always a "we" endeavor, not just a "me" enterprise. God designed us to contribute to the "we" relationships of our life.

How do you best contribute on a team? How do you make those around you better?

We all have strengths and needs in how we work on a team. The descriptive phrases we use in *"Your Leadership Grip"* give us a simple way to discern our strengths and needs:

Let's Go—usually the person leading a team toward a goal, setting or sharing a vision of "what could be." They are willing to take on big challenges, move quickly and take risks.

Let's Be Careful—helps the team pay attention to details, budget, policies and administrative issues. They are more deliberate, preferring to plan thoroughly and minimize risk.

Let Me Help You—loves to come alongside and serve or equip others. They are great at taking care of the practical and logistical needs of a team.

Let's Stay Together—values the relational health, chemistry and unity of the team. They are the honey and the glue of every team because they put relationships above all else.

Usually we are strong in a couple of these team styles and need help in one. For example, I'm a strong "Let's Go" and "Let Me Help You" person, but need a "Let's Be Careful" person with me on a team.

Coach Yourself Forward

Think about the teams you've been on. What are your strong team styles? Who do you need?

Often the people we need most also irritate us most because they are so different from us. A key principle here is; "Irritate or appreciate...it's up to you." How can you apply that principle on the teams you are a part of?

Some of us have a hard time admitting we need others. If that's you, go to the people who have been patient and helpful with you and thank them.

If you haven't taken the team style portion of the "Your Leadership Grip" or "Discovering Your Ministry Identity" by Paul Ford, plan to complete one of them (www.churchsmart.com or www.leadershipgrip.com). You'll be glad you did!

What inspiration are you hearing from others?

> Several years ago a twelve year old girl named Natalie
> Gilbert won a contest to sing the national anthem at an
> NBA playoff game. In front of over 18,000 amped up
> fans at the Rose Garden in Portland, Oregon, and two
> eager basketball teams, Natalie started singing "The
> Star Spangled Banner." A few lines into the song she
> faltered and stopped...she had forgotten the words!
> Jeers and cat calls began to rain down on her. Suddenly
> Mo Cheeks, coach of one of the teams, was standing
> alongside her, quietly urging, "Come on, come on," and
> helped her sing the phrase she had forgotten,
> "starlight's last gleaming." Smiling nervously, Natalie
> found her voice and began to sing the song she was
> meant to sing again...hesitantly, then with increasing
> confidence as Mo reminded her of the words. By the
> way, Mo can't sing well at all! Before she finished, the
> whole arena was singing along. Within days, the video
> went viral and a whole nation sang with her. [12]

God has created us with a voice to sing a unique song only we can
sing. It's intimately linked to His great purpose for us! We each get
to sing our God-designed song as part of His choir for His glory!
When we sing for Jesus, we sing the Salvation Song...the song our
whole world needs to hear! There's no greater joy than to know
that in singing our God song, we are helping others want to sing
the salvation song, too. That's when we truly fit and flourish.

God brings people into our lives to help us find our voice and sing
the song God created us to sing. They help us "when we forget the
words." They believe in us when others give up on us. They speak
encouragement, blessing and destiny to us. They remind us of
God's promises. They sometimes "call us out" in admonishment
and at the same time "call us up," exhorting us to live up to God's
high calling for us.

It's a sacred thing to recognize God speaking to us through others.
Their messages all fit a common theme the Lord wants us to hear.

Often they don't know each other and all they have in common is a relationship with us. They may not even realize that what they are saying is so important, but we recognize their words as inspiration from the Lord. It's as if the Holy Spirit is whispering, "Listen to them...I'm speaking to you through them!"

God provides people who inspire us in many ways...
Some do by <u>example</u>...they may be biblical, historical or current heroes.
Some do by <u>listening</u> to us...giving us the gift of a listening ear and heart.
Some do by <u>mentoring</u> us...they pour in wisdom and advice at just the right time while still keeping the focus on what we need, not what they want to tell.
Some do by <u>coaching</u> us...they draw out what God's doing, listening and asking in ways that help us focus, get a clear picture of reality, discern options and develop action steps that energize and empower us with hope.
Some do by <u>loving</u> us and <u>believing</u> in us at our lowest times, encouraging us to find fresh hope in the Lord.
Some do by <u>blessing</u> us with help, provision, protection or recommendation at just the right time.

There are many people who will criticize, question, belittle, discourage and use us. Rare are those who intentionally encourage, bless, uplift and make us better.

I have a few men in my life that I call "heart holders." They truly care for my soul. They want the best for me. They protect me. They speak truth with grace into my life, calling me out when I need it and always calling me up to God's best. They hold my heart and don't hurt it. Heart holders are rare...they are among God's most precious gifts to us. If you have one, thank God. Be a heart holder in return! If you don't, pray for one. Become one to others.

Coach Yourself Forward

Who are the people in your life who inspire you to discover and passionately pursue God's great purpose for your life? Make a list of them.

Although we mentioned this earlier, find a way to thank them soon...tell them how much they mean to you. Share with them specifically the ways they have helped you. If they are not alive anymore, find a member of their family and tell stories of how that person blessed you and made such a difference that you are telling stories about them years later! Gratitude keeps on giving!

How well do you inspire others? How much of your life is focused on you and your needs? What is the Lord saying to you about how He wants to cleanse your motives, adjust your priorities and intentionally bless others? How willing are you to allow Him to do whatever He wants so He can bless others through you?

Who can you become a heart holder for? Determine with God's help to become one of those rare people who are of great value in Heaven's eyes and the hearts of those you hold faithfully.

6
Look For
Identify Fruit, Promises, Doors

"The future is as bright as the promises of God."

"There are basically two ways to live: problem to problem or promise to promise."

"The best way to project future behavior is past performance."

What kind of fruit have you produced consistently?

"You can identify them by their fruit..." (Matthew 7:16, NLT)

Understanding the "fruit" God is bearing in and through is a wonderful part of your fit and flourish discernment process. Let's look at "fruit" from several different Biblical perspectives...

First, the fruit of <u>actions</u> in the form of our conduct, living a righteous life. *"Therefore produce fruit that proves repentance."* (Matthew 3:8) *"For the fruit of the light consists in all goodness, righteousness and truth..."* (Galatians 5:9) If our walk doesn't match our talk, we lose credibility. God can plant the seeds of His character, holy love, in our inward lives and then live His life through us so the outward fruit people see is the sweet, nourishing lifestyle that honors Jesus in all we do.

Second, the fruit of <u>attitudes</u> in the form of our character, the fruit of the Spirit. *"The fruit of the Spirit is love, joy, peace, patience, kindness, goodness, faithfulness, gentleness and self-control.... those who belong to Christ have crucified the sinful nature with its passions and desires. If we live by the Spirit, let us also keep in step with the Spirit."* (Galatians 5:21-25, NIV) If a righteous lifestyle that honors the Lord is the visible fruit people can see, the roots from which that fruit is nourished is the fruit of the Spirit. Christlike roots below, Christlike fruit above. My life verse is Isaiah 37:31: *"Take root below, bear fruit above..."* Love from a pure heart fuels a lifestyle evidenced by love's fruit in all its flavors.

Third, the fruit of additions to the Kingdom in the form of conversions, growing God's family. *"Those who accepted his message were baptized, and about 3,000 were added to their number that day...and the Lord added to their number daily those who were being saved." (Acts 2:42, 47, NIV)* Jesus' great "Go-mission" of Matthew 28:18-20 authorizes us in our daily lives by saying, "As you are going, make disciples..." Every one of us has a part in making disciples, adding to the family of God and expanding our Father King's rule and reign in hearts, families, neighborhoods, communities, regions and nations.

Here's where many people struggle...they don't think they have anything to contribute when it comes to seeing people coming to Christ. As a result, they don't feel very useful or valuable in the Lord's work. Yet, we all have an important part to play! Think of bringing people the Good News of Jesus (I like to call it "Good Newsing") in these three ways:

- It is supernatural. We get to cooperate with the Holy Spirit as He works in people's lives. He goes where we can't go, speaking to people in their hearts, drawing them in supernatural ways. We get to be His hands and feet and voice.
- It's a process. We are all on a spiritual journey. We get to come alongside people at a point on their spiritual journey. We meet them where they are and help them choose to move toward where God wants them to be.
- It's a team effort. We all have a part in God's miraculous redemptive work! If we think that only certain personalities, skills, gifts or styles—only "superstars"--can be used by God to bring others to know Him, we're not seeing the way God sees. It takes all kinds of people to reach all kinds of people...we are ALL a part of God's mission!

The apostle Paul gives us some helpful ways to see how we all contribute to fulfilling the great commission in I Corinthians 3:6: *"I planted the seed, Apollos watered it, but God made it grow." (NIV)*

Some are *"seed sowers."* They show the love of Jesus in practical ways...they show more than tell. Small but supernaturally powerful acts of kindness, service, encouragement, hospitality, listening and modeling the love of Jesus leave people with a lingering sense of the presence of Jesus wherever seed sowers go. Their alongside style and spiritual gifts like helps, mercy, service, giving, craftsmanship and encouragement all make both an initial and eternal difference! Because they are sowing seeds, and seeds take time to take root, they often don't realize how much influence they have. Yet, without seed sowers, there is no fruit later!

Some are *"next steppers."* They water the Gospel seeds by helping people take their next steps on their spiritual journey. They answer questions, bring understanding through teaching or preaching, pray with and for people powerfully and show up at Spirit-appointed times to enable people to take the next steps toward Jesus and with Jesus. Both upfront and alongside, their gifts of wisdom, teaching, faith, encouragement, words of knowledge and pastoring are used by the Holy Spirit to draw people to Christ.

Some are *"attending physicians."* These are the people with the gift of evangelism. They may also have gifts like leadership, faith, prophecy, healing and miracles. They have a supernatural way of being present and guiding people to make the decision to follow Christ as Savior. Remember, only God our Father saves...spiritual birth is a supernatural miracle from Him. However, He uses His "Good Newsers" to bring people to the point of decision and like an attending physician assist a healthy spiritual birth to happen.

We may take part in more than one of the aspects of Good Newsing others, but the end result is always seeing people come to know and follow Jesus. When that happens, we all rejoice...because we've all had a part...Heaven rejoices...God is glorified!

Fourth, there is the fruit of our <u>activities</u>, in the form of our competence, the skills we are good at. Throughout Scripture, we see men and women being described in terms of the skills where they excelled. Their competence brought forth the fruit of productive results in many beautiful ways. This is an oft-forgotten aspect of fruitfulness...we need to pay attention to what your fruit looks like in terms of ongoing skills and competence. It helps us answer the "how do you do that?" question as we help others discern their fit and flourish. "How do you lead?" "How do you bring others together?" "How do you create environments where people feel accepted and spiritual conversations happen safely?" We fit and flourish when we get to use do what we are good at for God's glory.

Actions...attitudes...additions...activities.
Conduct...character...conversions...competence.
All these are ways that you need to consider what "fruit" looks like in your life.

A great question to help you identify what kind of fruit you consistently produce is this: "What do others often say about *who you are* and *what you do* that God uses consistently to influence people for Him?"

Coach Yourself Forward

Review the four kinds of fruit we looked at Biblically. Where are you strong? Where are you weak? Who do you need? In what ways is the Lord at work in these areas?
   My conduct
   My character
   Helping others convert to Christ
   My competency and skills

Look at the different ways God uses us to "Good News" others. Which of these evangelism/"good newsing" styles—seed planting, next stepping, attending physician--is strongest for you? Who do you need to partner with to be even more effective? Thank God for your part in bringing people to Christ...and ask God for more opportunities!

Reflect on and answer the question we highlighted: *"What do people often say about who you are (your character) and what you do (your skills and gifts) that God uses consistently to influence people for Him?"* Ask your spouse and/or other significant people in your life to answer that question for you. Listen closely to what they have to say. They will have insights that will bring more clarity and blessing for you! Now, summarize all those thoughts and write them down.

What promises are you hearing from God?

You can choose to live one of two ways..."problem to problem" or "promise to promise." Which you choose dramatically affects your perspective, your attitudes, your walk with God and what He can do in and through you!

The Bible is many things. It's a love letter. It's a life guide. It's the written revelation of the Father, Son and Spirit. It trains us to know truth and live aligned with truth. It's a song book. It's a history book of HIS story and ours. It describes God's marvelous grace through the stories of lives across many generations, nations and cultures. It's timeless and timely wisdom. It's philosophy, psychology, sociology and many other "ologies" at the deepest level of human life. There is no other book like it today or in all human history. It stands alone as the divinely inspired, inerrant Word of God.

The Bible is also a promise book! Estimates about how many promises the Bible contains range from several thousand to 30,000. Someone counted 365 "fear not" promises...one for every day of the year! Some promises were intensely personal...for a particular person and time. Some of them are universal for all people for all generations. Some had a "near" fulfillment that also fore-shadow a "future" and ultimate fulfillment.

Learning to live "promise to promise" carries us through our dark discouraging times and lifts us upward to experience God's best in any situation. The apostle Peter was one who learned to live promise to promise. In II Peter, his letter to scattered, disenfranchised and persecuted believers, Peter begins by reinforcing the joy of promise to promise living:

> *"Simon Peter, a servant and apostle of Jesus Christ, to those who through the righteousness of our God and Savior Jesus Christ have received a faith as precious as ours: Grace and peace be yours in abundance through the knowledge of God and of Jesus our Lord. His divine*

*power has given us everything we need for a godly life
through our knowledge of him who called us by his own
glory and goodness. Through these he has given us his
very great and precious promises, so that through them
you may participate in the divine nature, having escaped
the corruption in the world caused by evil desires."*

(I Peter 1:1-4)

In these verses, we learn the wonderful design of God's promises. His promises are:

Purchased by Christ Jesus. *"...given to us"* (v. 3, 4) Jesus paid for God's promises...we don't earn them.

Received and activated by faith. *"...received a faith..."* (v. 2) It's not the size of our faith but the size of our God that makes the difference.

Opportunities for God to reveal Himself. *"...knowledge of Him"* (v. 2) When we activate God's promises, He can reveal Himself in many, powerful beautiful ways.

Minister to the heart needs of people. *"...everything we need"* (v. 3) God's promises apply to all of life!

Involves us in cooperating with God! *"...participate..."* (v. 4) God has the power, we get to be His partner!

Stimulates our vision. *"...abundance...for life and godliness..."* (v. 2, 3) We can claim great promises because we have a great God!

Expands the Kingdom of God! *"...His glory..."* (v. 3) When God fulfills His promises, it glorifies Him and draws others to know Him.

Even better than the promises we find in Scripture is the One who gives them! He is the Promise Maker and Promise Keeper. He will give you promises that encourage, sustain and empower you every step of the way as you journey with Him. Here are some different ways you can live "promise to promise." Remember, God wants to share His promises with you, so don't be afraid to ask Him! You will often discover that you don't have to search for God's promises... they will find you as you spend time in His Word and listen to the Holy Spirit.

A *"life verse"* is a promise that you receive for a lifetime...it becomes your theme and dream from Him. A life verse shapes identity and destiny. My life verse is "...*take root below, bear fruit above*..." from Isaiah 37:31. It informs one of my life principles: "I am responsible for the depth of my relationship with God. He is responsible for the breadth of my influence for Him."

A *"year verse"* is a promise for a year or a period of time. It holds us steady in tough times and encourages to believe God for His best. It is amazing how the Holy Spirit will remind us of that promise at just the right time. Sometimes a particular promise will stay with us for a season of our lives.

A *"promise for the day"* will come from your regular time in the Word. Rather than trying to remember everything you read on a given day, ask the Lord for a promise for that day. It may be just a single word, a phrase, an entire verse or a passage. Throughout that day, you can return to that promise over and over again. Rather than just allowing your mind to shift into "neutral" in the small spaces of your day (such as waiting at a stop light, standing in a line, walking from one place to another, during commercials on TV, etc.), you can return to the promise of the day and have it feed and strengthen you.

Here's a simple way to activate a promise for your day:

> *Promise* from the Word. The Lord will show it to you.
> *Pen* it. Write it down where you can easily see it and carry it with you.
> *Personalize* it. Deliberately make it yours...claim it for yourself.
> *Pray* it. Lift it up to the Lord as a promise from Him...and receive it as a gift from Him!
> *Praise* it! Declare the promise in the authority of the Lord.
> *Practice* it. Find ways to apply that promise as you go about your day.
> *Pass* it on! Share the promise with others...invite them to make it theirs, too!

A *"just-in-time promise."* Often we are caught by surprise by a circumstance, temptation or opportunity. In that instant, the Lord our Promise Giver will give you a promise that perfectly fits your need. Storing many promises in your heart allows the Holy Spirit to remind you of just the right promise at just the right time in just the right way.

As you can see, God's promises come in a myriad of ways and can be activated in many ways. If we are willing and intentional, you'll find that the Lord is eager to help you live a life of vibrant trust and confidence in Him and His promises...promise-to-promise living!

As you discern your fit and flourish life, listen for God's promises. Weave them into the rhythm of your life. Expect them! Activate them!

Coach Yourself Forward

Do you tend to live more "problem to problem" or "promise to promise"? Why?

What is your understanding about the nature of God's promises? How does how you see God, as we talked about earlier, affect the way you view His promises?

What did you learn about activating promises that you will apply to your spiritual rhythms?

What promises are you hearing from the Lord right now? How do they fit into your understanding of what fit and flourish looks like for you?

Arrow

"He made me into a sharpened arrow..."
(Isaiah 49:2, NET)

I still don't know what He saw in me.

I was just another stone, a nondescript pebble in the midst of many similar stones scattered in the bottom of the brook.

I was not beautifully colored with intricate designs so as to capture anyone's eye with my natural attractiveness.

I was not large, demanding attention by the sheer heft of my bulk.

No....I was just one chip off a rock, a simple singular stone seemingly of no significance.

Until....
    until *He* saw me and picked me up and claimed me
        for His own.

He took me home with Him, and once there He put me among a number of other pebbles, some in their original form...
    and others showing evidence that He had begun to work
        on them.

Those stones had begun to show potential beyond just being a shapeless and seemingly useless chunk of rock. It was obvious He had a purpose for them, and I began to wonder for the first time if He had a purpose for me, too.

And then....He began to work on me.

At first I had no idea what He was trying to do. He clamped me firmly in place, restricting my freedom and yet putting me exactly where He wanted me. It was somewhat uncomfortable and yet I did not feel constricted.

Somehow, because I was in His control, I knew I would be all right.

He was deliberate, careful and intentional as He started to shape me. It was obvious He saw something in me that I didn't...something that required that He chip away all of me that was not essential to His purposes.

And so, hammer and hardened chisel in hand, He began to fashion me, working from a vision and a blueprint that He had in His heart.

It was sometimes painful....
    painful because I was so dull and there was so much
        of me that He didn't need to fulfill His purpose. He
            hammered away at me at times, with splinters
                and sparks flying in all directions.

There were times when I thought I'd break in a thousand pieces and not survive the process.

Yet...
    yet He always knew where to apply the chisel of His
        purpose, always according to His blueprint and
            always with perfect timing.

There were times when things seemed exceedingly, excruciatingly slow.

He would take me and put me up against a grindstone and grind away at the rough edges. Sometimes He would use other stones like coarse sandpaper to do the job, and some rubbed the wrong way. It was tedious, but necessary for the transformation He had in mind.

I could tell He was willing to take the time to do the job right. Still, I wondered if He was really making any progress much less nearing a finished product. I learned that my sense of time and His timing were not always in synch. Now I know that His ways are much higher than my ways, and infinitely better.

Slowly (and in my eyes miraculously) I began to see that the shape of His vision for me become *my* shape in His hands.

The unnecessary parts were chipped away...
   the rough edges made smooth,
     the smooth edges honed until they became pointed
       and sharp.

It was then that at last I could see what He had seen in me all along.

I, the nondescript, insignificant pebble among many
   had become a polished arrow, fit for His purposes.

He might use me as a means of provision, becoming the instrument through which He could supply the needs of many people.

He might use me as a weapon of warfare, through which He could protect the weak or overcome the enemy in a display of His strength.

He might use me to drive home the point of His truth in the heart of a target of His choosing.

It doesn't matter how He uses me, as long as I am in His hands, at His disposal and available for His purpose....

because once I was shapeless...
>pointless....
>>useless.

But now...
>now I am sharp.
>>Polished.
>>>Ready.

I am an arrow ready in my Master's hand.

Wherever His will directs me and His strength delivers
>me, I will go, right to the heart of His divine purpose
>>for me.

I am an arrow...
>ready in my Master's hand.

--Tim Roehl

It's humbling to realize how intentional, purposeful and very personal God is as He stretches, shapes and sharpens us for His great purposes. We are that important to Him! There's always room to grow and become more like Jesus, but the Lord will deliberately shape and sharpen us at each stage of our journey for how He wants to work in and through us.

Look for the ways God is at work making you into His "sharpened arrow." He may be stretching your faith to trust Him in ways you haven't before. He might be shaping your character so people see more of Jesus in you. He might be sharpening us by chipping away our own preferences, comforts and methods. What may not make sense now will often become supernaturally clear later. As we submit to His sovereign sharpening process, trusting Him with what we do not know, we live in the present with our hearts preparing for the future.

Often we'll need the good help of mentors and coaches to help us process what God is doing. They can lead us to discover insights, promises to claim, perspective that brings hope and possible steps forward. My working definition of hope is "a view of tomorrow that makes today worth living."

Live in hope as the Lord works!

Don't shortcut God's sharpening!

Coach Yourself Forward

As you read the "Arrow" reflection, how does it resonate with your own experience?

How has the Lord stretched, shaped and sharpened you in the past?

What areas of your life is the Lord stretching, shaping and sharpening now?

Who are the people you can turn to for perspective, support, prayer and challenge as the Lord is doing His work making you into His "sharpened arrow"? When and how will you spend time with them?

What doors might God be opening for you?

"I will make the Valley of Achor (trouble) _a door of hope_ and expectation [anticipating the time when I will restore My favor on her.]" (Hosea 2:15, AMP 2015)

"Ask and it will be given to you; seek and you will find; knock and _the door will be opened for you_...for everyone who asks receives; he who seeks finds; and to him who knocks, the door will be opened." (Matthew 7:7,8 NIV)

"Pray for me because _a door for effective work has opened to me_, and there are many who oppose me." (I Corinthians 16:9, NIV)

"And pray for us, too, _that God may open a door_ for our message." (Colossians 4:3, NIV)

"I know your deeds. See, _I have placed before you an open door_ that no one can shut. I know that you have little strength, yet you have kept My word and have not denied my name." (Revelation 3:8, NIV)

"Here I am! _I stand at the door and knock_. If anyone hears My voice and opens the door, I will come in and eat with him (make Myself at home with you), and he with Me." (Revelation 3:20, NIV, Tim Roehl)

"That night Paul had a dream: A Macedonian stood on the far shore and called across the sea, 'Come over to Macedonia and help us!' _The dream gave Paul his map_. We went to work at once getting things ready to cross over to Macedonia. All the pieces had come together. We knew now for sure that God had called us to preach the good news to the Europeans."
(Acts 16:9-10, The Message)

When it comes to ways we can serve the Lord, the opportunities are unlimited! While the options are many, the ways we best fit and flourish to serve the Lord most fruitfully will be reduced by the Lord to a focused few. Paul Ford's "65/35 principle" reminds us that we are all called to be servants who are willing to serve however and wherever the Lord might want, even where we may not have gifts, skills or passion for that work. We can do that best if it doesn't require the majority of our time and energy, represented by the "35." However, we are also believing that the Lord wants to steward our life so that we are able to give the majority of our time --our "65"—where our personality, gifts, skills, passion and sense of calling fit and flourish for maximum Kingdom impact.

The more we understand how the Lord has made us to fit and flourish, the more we'll recognize the doors that represent His fit and flourish leading.

How do we recognize God's fit and flourish doors? You can find some practical principles in the outline called *"Seven Checks to Discern God's Will"* in the appendix of this book. Interestingly, however, we often don't need to search desperately for God's open doors. He opens them in His timing, and His timing is perfect. In my own journey, I have often been restless as I realized that God was preparing me to walk through an open door. The preparation, however, usually takes much longer than I thought it would!

So, instead of searching to find God's doors of opportunity, do what the Lord spoke clearly to me during a time of waiting: "Be faithful and grateful where you are...I'll open the door when it's time." Serve with joy and faithfulness where you are. When God's timing is right, He will open a door that is so clear it will be unmistakable for you...

A call from "out of the blue," completely unforeseen but obviously orchestrated by God. ..

An unexpected meeting with someone that has all the earmarks of being a divine appointment. ..

Divine delays that slow us down so we are in the right place

when God swings open a divine door. Closed doors that
disappoint us initially but replaced with better doors
that amaze and delight.

A pressing need that calls to you...and you realize that
God has uniquely prepared you for such a time as this!

The invitation may come in any one of a variety of ways, but you'll
recognize God's voice reassured with His peace. As Isaiah of old
heard, you'll also hear, *"Whether you turn to the right or to the
left, your ears will hear a voice behind you, saying, **This is the way;**
walk in it."* (Isaiah 30:21, emphasis added)

Coach Yourself Forward

As you read the verses talking about doors, which of them stood
out to you most? What do you sense the Lord might be saying to
you through them?

"Be grateful and faithful where you are...I'll open the door when
it's time." In what ways might the Lord be calling you to stay where
you are right now, being grateful and faithful?

How has the Lord opened doorways for you in the past? What did
you learn from those experiences that have prepared you for His
open doors now?

What doorways are you aware of right now? In our Appendix, walk
through the "Seven Checks to Discerning God's Will" and look at
those doors through the lens of the seven checks. What clarity
does that bring? What further questions does it raise? Lay them
before the Lord in prayer.

7

Look Out

The Call to a Heart for the World

Do you see what I see?
Do you hear what I hear?
Do you feel what I feel?
Will you go where I go?
Will you go with Me?
...God

In the United States, we live in an "80-80-80-80-2-1" reality...

80% of Americans are unchurched
80% of American churches are plateaued or in decline
80% of unchurches people say they would be interested in visiting a church if invited by a friend
80% of Christians never invite anyone to come to church with them
Only 2% of Christians ever invited an unchurched friend to come to church with them
Only 1% of all income in American churches goes to reach people for Christ around the world

How comfortable are you with that reality?

"We put our YES! on the table...God puts it on the map."
—Ed Stetzer

"Here am I! Send me!"
(Isaiah in Isaiah 6:8)

See: How can you see through God's eyes and get God's heart for the world?

How big is your world?

How big is your heart for the people of the world Jesus loves?

Your world can be as small as you and your own wants and needs. Your world might include your family and close friends. Think of it as you standing in a small circle. The circle marks your boundaries.

That's a pretty small world.

Or… you can remove your boundaries…open your heart wide…see the world as God sees it…get a heart like His as big as the world He loves and wants to redeem!

Your heart for God's world can reach across the street or to the ends of the earth. It can yearn to see a continual stream of people far from God come home to be redemptively reunited with their Heavenly Father.

Most Jesus followers really don't want to be in the selfish confines of living only for themselves. They want a heart like God's that loves lost people like He does and want to be a part of fulfilling God's Great Co-Mission. Is that "ideal" or "real" for you?

How can you see through the Lord's eyes and get His heart for a lost world?

See by the Numbers

Fair warning: if you are not a "numbers" person, the next section may make your eyes glaze over. While numbers can't tell the whole story, they help us see an important part of reality. My goal in quoting so many statistics is make us more aware and hopefully raise our level of urgency about the needs of our world. When you look at the world "by the numbers," you begin to see immense needs and opportunities...

How many people are there in God's world?

There are 7.3 billion people in the world. (Joshua Project)

- Median age – total: 28.4 years
- Life expectancy – total population: 67.07 years

Top Ten Countries by Population: (in millions, July 2011, CIA world factbook)

- China 1,336.72
- India 1,189.17
- United States 313.23
- Indonesia 245.61
- Brazil 203.43
- Pakistan 187.34
- Bangladesh 158.57
- Nigeria 155.22
- Russia 138.74
- Japan 126.48

What do they believe?

Population by Religion:

- 2.3 billion are Christian (748 million are evangelical Christians). (Joshua Project; Barrett and Johnson 2001, 20)
- 1.7 billion are Muslim. (Joshua Project)
- 1.1 billion are Hindu. (Joshua Project)
- 979 million are Non-Religious. (Joshua Project)
- 671 million are of Ethnic Religions including Chinese Religion. (Joshua Project)
- 488 million are Buddhist. (Joshua Project)
- 103 million other/unknown. (Joshua Project)
- Of the 7.3 billion people in the world, 3 billion live among unreached people groups of the world and 1.6 billion are completely unevangelized. (Joshua Project; Barrett and Johnson 2001, 427)

There are 6,510 languages in the world. (Joshua Project)

People groups are what Bible scholars believe are referred to in many mission-oriented verses, such as Matthew 28:19, 24:14, and Revelation 7:9. According to one database, there are 16,700 people groups in the world. Of these people groups, 9,715 have been reached with the Gospel message while 6,847 people groups are still unreached. "Unreached" means less than 2% are Evangelical Christian, the proportional size thought to be needed to reach their own people. (Joshua Project)

86% of all unreached people groups lie within the region called the 10/40 window, which is between 10 and 40 degrees north and from the west coast of Africa to the east coast of Asia. (Joshua Project)

In the last 40 years, over one billion people have died who have never heard of Jesus, and around 30 million people this year will perish without hearing the message of salvation. (Baxter 2007, 12)

70,000+ people die every day in the unreached world without Jesus. (Baxter 2007, 12)

60% of unreached people groups live in countries closed to missionaries from North America. (The Traveling Team)

God's moving people all over the world ...and bringing the world to our door in the US!

22 million internationals visit the US each year. Of these, some 630,000 are university students from 220 countries, 25% of which prohibit Christian missionaries. 80% of those students will return to their countries having never been invited to an American home. (The Traveling Team)

40% of the world's 220 Heads of State once studied in the US. (The Traveling Team). 60% of international students come from the 10/40 window. 90% of international students are unreached by ministries while in the United States. (The Traveling Team)

The number of people migrating from one place in the world for different reasons is increasing dramatically. This movement provides unprecedented opportunities to be the hands and feet of Jesus and share the Good News of the salvation of Jesus.

How well is God's Church reaching the world?

In AD 100 there were 360 people for every believer. Now there are about 9.5 people for every evangelical believer. (Winter et al., 1)

In AD 100 there were 12 unreached people groups for every congregation of believers. Now there is 1 unreached people group for every 1000 congregations. (Winter et al., 3)

Over 160,000 believers will be martyred this year. (The Traveling Team)

90% of foreign missionaries work among already reached people groups. 10% work among unreached people groups. (Winter and Koch, 543)

Of the more than 70,000 North American missionaries, only 5,000 are working among the totally unreached people. (Yohannan, Revolution in World Missions, 154)

There are around 285,000 indigenous (aka national, native, home) missionaries serving in the world. They make up 2/3 of the world's missionary force. (Yohannan, Come Let's Reach the World, 23)

86 countries prohibit or restrict Western missionaries. (Yohannan, Come Let's Reach the World, 31)

The potential audience for Christian radio programming is 99% of the world's population, assuming good reception, availability of a radio and a desire to find the programs. (Johnstone and Mandryk 2005, 7)

Two of the largest Gospel radio broadcasters, Far East Broadcasting Company and Gospel for Asia, both receive around 1,000,000 listener responses each year. (Far East Broadcasting Company, 15; Gospel for Asia)

Despite Christ's command to evangelize, 67% of all humans from AD 30 to the present day have never even heard the name of Jesus Christ. (Baxter 2007, 12)

91% of all Christian outreach/evangelism does not target non-Christians, but targets other Christians. (Baxter 2007, 12)

Christian Workers
- Full time Christian Workers in the World : 5.5 million workers
- Christian workers in the Reached World : 4.19 million local workers (75.9%)
- Christian workers in the Unevangelized : 1.3 million local workers (23.7%)
- Christian workers in the Unreached : 20,500 local workers (0.37%)

Missionaries Per Religion
- Tribal – 714,108,000 population with 11,900 Missionaries: 1 for every 60,000
- Hindus – 984,532,000 population with 5,500 Missionaries: 1 for every 179,000
- Unreligious – 831,267,000 population with 11,700 Missionaries: 1 for every 71,000
- Muslims – 1,703,146,000 population with 4,200 Missionaries: 1 for every 405,500
- Buddhists – 520,002,000 population with 2,000 Missionaries: 1 for every 260,000

Unreached People Groups:
- Total People Groups: 16,750
- Total Unreached People Groups: 6,921
- Total Population of UPGs: 2.84 billion people
- Total Percentage of world: UPG's make up 40.6% of world population

Where Does Our Money Go?

The average American Christian gives only 1 penny a day to global missions. (Yohannan, Revolution in World Missions, 142)

Only .1% (that's one tenth of one percent) of all Christian giving is directed toward mission efforts in the 38 most unevangelized countries in the world. (Barrett and Johnson 2001, 656)

Christians spend more on the annual audits of their churches and agencies ($810 million) than on all their workers in the non-Christian world. (World Evangelization Research Center)

American Christians spend 95% of offerings on home-based ministry, 4.5% on cross-cultural efforts in already reached people groups, and .5% to reach the unreached. (The Traveling Team)

Christians make up 33% of the world's population, but receive 53% of the world's annual income and spend 98% of it on themselves. (Barrett and Johnson 2001, 656)

Approximately 85% of all missionary finances are being used by Western missionaries who are working among the established churches on the field rather than being used for pioneer evangelism to the lost. (Yohannan, Revolution in World Missions, 143)

Indigenous missionaries do 90% of pioneer mission work, but only receive 10% of mission funding. Meanwhile foreign missionaries do 10% of pioneer mission work, but receive 90% of mission funding. (Finley 2004, 178 & 244)

Spending Priorities of the Church in the USA:
- 85% of all funding goes towards internal operations
- 50% to pay the salary of pastors and church staff.
- 22% to pay for upkeep and expansion of buildings.
- 13% for church expenses such as electricity and supplies.
- 15% for outreach includes 3% for local missions.
- 2% for overseas missions (both evangelistic and charitable)

- In the end, if you only give to your local church, odds are that only 2% of 2.58%, or 0.05% of your income is going towards "preaching the gospel to every nation" and helping the "poorest of the poor" combined. To put that in perspective, if you make $50,000 a year, that is only $25.80 per year.
- American Christians spend 95% of offerings on home-based ministry, 4.5% on cross-cultural efforts in already reached people groups, and .5% to reach the unreached. (The Traveling Team)
- Annual income of all church members: $30.5 trillion.
- Annual income of Evangelical Christians is approximately $6.72 trillion.
- Given to any Christian causes: $545 billion (1.8% of our income). That's also how much we spend in America on Christmas!
- Given to Missions: $31 billion, (0.1%). That's only 5.7% of the money given to Christian causes of any kind. That's also how much we spend in America on dieting programs.
- Money that goes toward the Reached world: $26,970,000,000 (that means 87% of the money given to "Missions" goes to areas with "reached" status or access to the gospel already).
- Money that goes toward Unreached Peoples: $310 million (that's only 1% of what is given to "Missions."). That's also how much Americans in 2011 spent on Halloween costumes (for their pets).
- The $310 million (going toward Unreached People Group's) is only .001% of the $30.5 trillion Income of Christians. (for every $100,000 that Christians make, they give $1 to the unreached.)

Think About It:

Evangelical Christians could provide all of the funds needed to plant a church in each of the 6,900 unreached people groups with only 0.03% of their income.

The Church has roughly 3,000 times the financial resources and 9,000 times the manpower needed to finish the Great Commission. If every evangelical gave 10% of their income to missions we could easily support two million new missionaries.
(From www.thetravelingteam.org)

(All reference sources located in Endnote section.[15-29])

An Orchard Parable: The Society for the Picking of Apples

A missions parable about lost people: putting world evangelism statistics in perspective by James M. Weber, missionary to Japan

Are you familiar with the parable Jesus told about the lost sheep? Here's one on a similar note except that it's about the ruined apples from a potentially plentiful harvest.

Once upon a time there was an apple grower who had acres and acres of apple trees. In all, he had 10,000 acres of apple orchards.

One day he went to the nearby town. There, he hired 1,000 apple pickers. He told them:

"Go to my orchards. Harvest the ripe apples, and build storage buildings for them so that they will not spoil. I need to be gone for a while, but I will provide all you will need to complete the task. When I return, I will reward you for your work.

"I'll set up a Society for the Picking of Apples. The Society--to which you will all belong--will be responsible for the entire operation. Naturally, in addition to those of you doing the actual harvesting, some will carry supplies, others will care for the physical needs of the group, and still others will have administrative responsibilities."

As he set up the Society structure, some people volunteered to be pickers and others to be packers. Others put their skills to work as truck drivers, cooks, accountants, storehouse builders, apple inspectors and even administrators. Every one of his workers could, of course, have picked apples. In the end, however, only 100 of the 1,000 employees wound up as full-time pickers.

The 100 pickers started harvesting immediately. Ninety-four of them began picking around the homestead. The remaining six looked out toward the horizon. They decided to head out to the faraway orchards.

Before long, the storehouses in the 800 acres immediately surrounding the homestead had been filled by the 94 pickers with beautiful, delicious apples.

The orchards on the 800 acres around the homestead had thousands of apple trees. But with almost all of the pickers concentrating on them, those trees were soon picked nearly bare. In fact, the ninety-four apple pickers working around the homestead began having difficulty finding trees which had not been picked.

As the apple picking slowed down around the homestead, Society members began channeling effort into building larger storehouses and developing better equipment for picking and packing. They even started some schools to train prospective apple pickers to replace those who one day would be too old to pick apples.

Sadly, those ninety-four pickers working around the homestead began fighting among themselves. Incredible as it may sound, some began stealing apples that had already been picked. Although there were enough trees on the 10,000 acres to keep every available worker busy, those working nearest the homestead failed to move into unharvested areas. They just kept working those 800 acres nearest the house. Some on the northern edge sent their trucks to get apples on the southern side. And those on the south side sent their trucks to gather on the east side.

Even with all that activity, the harvest on the remaining 9,200 acres was left to just six pickers. Those six were, of course, far too few to gather all the ripe fruit in those thousands of acres. So, by the hundreds of thousands, apples rotted on the trees and fell to the ground.

One of the students at the apple-picking school showed a special talent for picking apples quickly and effectively. When he heard about the thousands of acres of untouched faraway orchards, he started talking about going there.

His friends discouraged him. They said: *"Your talents and abilities make you very valuable around the homestead. You'd be wasting your talents out there. Your gifts can help us harvest apples from the trees on our central 800 acres more rapidly. That will give us more time to build bigger and better storehouses. Perhaps you could even help us devise better ways to use our big storehouses since we have wound up with more space than we need for the present crop of apples."*

With so many workers and so few trees, the pickers and packers and truck drivers--and all the rest of the Society for the Picking of Apples living around the homestead -- had time for more than just picking apples. With so many workers and so few trees, the pickers and packers and truck drivers--and all the rest of the Society for the Picking of Apples living around the homestead--had time for more than just picking apples.

They built nice houses and raised their standard of living. Some became very conscious of clothing styles. Thus, when the six pickers from the far-off orchards returned to the homestead for a visit, it was apparent that they were not keeping up with the styles in vogue with the other apple pickers and packers.

To be sure, those on the homestead were always good to those six who worked in the far away orchards. When any of those six returned from the far away fields, they were given the red carpet treatment. Nonetheless, those six pickers were saddened that the Society of the Picking of Apples spent 96 percent of its budget for bigger and better apple-picking methods and equipment and personnel for the 800 acres around the homestead while it spent only four percent of its budget on all those distant orchards.

To be sure, those six pickers knew that an apple is an apple wherever it may be picked. They knew that the apples around the homestead were just as important as apples far away. Still, they could not erase from their minds the sight of thousands of trees which had never been touched by a picker.

They longed for more pickers to come help them. They longed for help from packers, truck drivers, supervisors, equipment-maintenance men and ladder builders. They wondered if the professionals working back around the homestead could teach them better apple-picking methods so that, out where they worked, fewer apples would rot and fall to the ground.

While one might question whether the Society was doing all the owner wanted done, the members did keep very busy. Several members were convinced that proper apple picking requires nothing less than the very best equipment. Thus, the Society assigned several members to develop bigger and better ladders as well as nicer boxes to store apples. The Society also prided itself at having raised the qualification level for full-time apple pickers.

Those six sometimes wondered to themselves whether or not the Society for the Picking of Apples was doing what the orchard owner had asked it to do.

When the owner returns, the Society members will crowd around him. They'll proudly show off the bigger and better ladders they've built and the nice apple boxes they've designed and made. One wonders how happy that owner will be when he looks out and sees the acres and acres of untouched trees with their unpicked apples.[30]

Coach Yourself Forward

When you look at the world, what do you "see"?

As we looked at the needs of the world "by the numbers," which of those statistics grabbed your attention? Why?

Who else has been noticing some of the same issues you have? How could you learn more about these needs together?

Who is doing something to meet the needs you were drawn to?

What ministries could you learn about that could be an option for you to partner with?

~NOTES~

Feel: What needs in our world stir passion in you?

Yearning for Shawn

When Shawn and his family moved across the street from us, it wasn't long before I learned two things: Shawn didn't care much for religion and God gave me a burden for Shawn.

I regularly prayed for my neighbors, but for some reason I found myself praying especially for Shawn...earnestly for Shawn.

When we connected as neighbors and I mentioned anything spiritual, I got a figurative stiff arm from Shawn letting me know he wasn't interested. Rather than giving up on my resistant friend, the Lord intensified my burden for him. I found myself praying for Shawn and his family at unusual and unexpected times—waking up in the night praying for him, on a flight at 30,000 feet, in my quiet times. I didn't just pray for Shawn, I *yearned* for Shawn to come to Christ.

Outwardly, nothing appeared to change. Time passed. I kept praying.

One day Shawn told me that he and his wife were getting a divorce. I ached for the pain his family was experiencing. I prayed even more for him. The pain opened doors for conversation as I asked what I could do to help. He thanked me when I said I was praying for him.

Another woman came into Shawn's life and she was spiritually curious. In spite of himself, Shawn listened in and engaged as Leann and I talked while we watched a basketball game at his house.

> More conversations...more yearning in prayer...and one night Shawn and Leann came to Christ in their living room. I performed their wedding not long after. They are following Jesus. Eight years of yearning prayer was worth it!
>
> -Tim Roehl

Here's a key truth about getting a heart for lost people...
Numbers must become names!

Statistics can be informative, insightful, overwhelming, even manipulated...but rarely do they generate passion and action. For that to happen, numbers must become names. Information must be identified and infused with the pain of real people. Passion then becomes personalized.

The story of my neighbor Shawn is an example. As a pastor, I knew all the statistics about unchurched people in my area and the theological importance of the Great Commission. The burden the Lord gave me for Shawn made all the impersonal statistics and theological statements become urgent, passionate and personal.

Who do you ache for...
  who do you weep for...
    who do you cry out to God, longing for them to come home?

Sometimes God gives us a passion and sense of calling not just to a person, but to a people group in a particular area or with a particular need.

> *At a One Weekend event we do at OMS, a young man named Robbie began to tell his story. He described being a young Christian who loved Jesus but was kind of drifting without a specific sense of purpose or passion. One day as he was channel surfing, he came across a TV program about a community devastated by a natural disaster. It struck him that the people of that community faced their*

> *futures without any sense of hope. Their hopelessness touched him deeply. "I wonder where these people live," he thought. When he found out these people were from Japan, he suddenly found himself weeping with a deep burden to bring the hope of Jesus to the people of Japan.*
>
> *As Robbie told that story to our group, he began to weep again. He testified that God had given him a purpose and passion for Japan. He was no longer drifting...he had direction!*

What touches you deeply at the level of your feelings? Even more...what makes you ache deeply on a heart level? What stirs such passion deep within that you have to act....have to!

Pay attention to where God is stirring this kind of passion in you...

A specific person...

A particular people group...

A group of people with specific needs...

Injustice on a personal or institutional level...

A growing sense of burden that leads you to exclaim, "Somebody's got to do something about this!"

Often you'll hear the quiet voice of the Holy Spirit saying, "What about you? I'm calling you." Often your own story—the places of pain and brokenness or sin you've gone through—has prepared you to meet those needs.

"The place God calls you to the place where your deep gladness and the world's deep hunger meet."
        — Frederick Buechner, Wishful Thinking: A Theological ABC

The place where you fit and flourish personally will intersect with the needs of people Jesus connects you to that He wants to redeem, restore and reconcile. You will make the transition from, "Somebody's got to do something about this!" to "I was made for this!"

Coach Yourself Forward

Who do you long to see come to Christ? If you don't have a list of people you are intentionally praying for, serving and loving for their sake and Jesus' sake, make one now. Let the Holy Spirit give you the names on *His* list He wants to put *your* on list.

What burdens you? Consider regions of the world, particular nations, people groups, people affected by an injustice or people with specific needs? Who do you know personally that "puts a name to the need"? Write down those names. If you don't have any, ask the Lord to help you find some!

Who do you know that is already meeting those needs? What people, organization and ministry agencies could you learn more about? Do some research and see where it leads.

Pray: How are you praying for people to come to Christ?

> "Before you talk to people about God,
> talk to God about those people."

> "Prayer is not overcoming God's reluctance...
> it is laying hold of God's willingness."

> "If you want to increase your harvest,
> you've got to intensify your intercession."

Learn about every great move of God in history--where multitudes of people came to Christ and Christians received a fresh infusion of holy love and passion for people far from God--and you'll find they began with a growing grassroots movement of passionate, intentional, intensely increasing intercession.

When you see God's world through His eyes...
  when you feel the needs of people He loves and longs for...
    you'll pray!

Intentional intercession on behalf of others blends adoration and intimacy with the Lord while also advocating on behalf of others and powerfully declaring our victory in Jesus, taking authority in His name.

Adoration...advocating...authority. This is the kind of prayer that influences history and the destiny of others.

How do you pray on behalf of others?

There is a wealth of tremendous prayer resources available to help us pray for the world intentionally. Authors like Dr. Wesley Duewel (who I got to know personally at the end of his life—at 99 years old he was still glowing and vibrant for Jesus and passionate to pray for the world) and Dick Eastman blend the passion of prayer and the practice of intentional intercession in such a way that my heart is ignited for God and I can't help but pray more!

"Igniting An Impassioned Prayer Life: How to Develop the Energized, Extended, and Sustainable Life of Prayer You've Always Wanted" by my friend Tom Stuart is another great example of a resource that helps you pray with more intentionality and Intimacy.

A "World Prayer Map" put out by Every Home for Christ helps me pray for every nation in the world every month.[31] It shows all 228 nations in the world, how many people live there, their nation's leader, whether it is a communist or restricted access country and what percentage of the people are evangelical Christians. One day I began counting the nations with few people who know Jesus. I counted 105 nations where less than 5% know Christ...and 78 where less than 2% know Jesus! I also found over 40 nations that are closed to Christian missionaries! These numbers spur my heart to pray even more!

There are lots of ways to pray...*how* you pray often depends on a number of factors, such as...
- How you best connect to and relate to the Lord
- What time of day allows you to meet Him when you are at your best
- Your life situation and schedule
- Your own spiritual disciplines and personal discipline
- Your willingness to invest in your relationship with the Lord
- Your passion to stand in the gap on behalf of others who need Jesus

...but the biggest questions are:

"What does your prayer life look like?"

"In what ways are you intentionally interceding for those the Lord has invited you to pray for?

Coach Yourself Forward

How can you strengthen prayer life?

Who are you praying for that needs Jesus?

What prayer resources have been helpful to you?

Who can you pray with for the sake of people who need Jesus?

Serve: How are you involved?

Ever heard of "zap theology"?

Let me describe it to you. Some people believe that God has called them to minister in another place (either in their homeland or another nation in the world)...and when they travel to that place, God will suddenly "zap" them with spiritual maturity, purity, authority and ability.

There is a bit of truth to that kind of thinking...an old axiom says, "God doesn't call the qualified, He qualifies the called." God does give supernatural provision to us...our weakness infused with His strength! When it happens, it makes us humble and grateful.

However there's another side to that story. If you are waiting to serve, (using your gifts and abilities in ministry and reach people for Christ) until you get to your "mission field," chances are you won't do it there...because you're not doing it here.

So...how are you currently serving Jesus and others? If you're waiting to know more, become more mature, have the ideal situation, get more training...there will always be a reason to wait.

As God helps you <u>see</u> needs around you...
   as God helps you <u>feel</u> the needs of others and you feel "their ache in your heart"...
     as the Holy Spirit is leading you to <u>pray</u> passionately on their behalf...
     then, make yourself available...go...ask how you can help...
     <u>serve</u>!

Watch how God uses you and grows your influence for Him as you do. There are needs that God created you to help meet! People are far more open to be listened to, loved, served and hear about Jesus than we give them credit for. Pastors and ministry leaders are often longing for more people to ask how the can be involved in ministry and serve with them.

Often we find our "fit and flourish" by experiencing many opportunities to serve and noticing where we experience God's power, joy and fruit as we do.

Always have a servant's heart...but you'll make your greatest Kingdom contribution when you fit and flourish. The journey to a fit and flourish begins with many small steps of service.

Coach Yourself Forward

How are you involved in helping fulfil God's Great Commission right now?

What has hindered you getting involved in serving others in Jesus' name in that past? What might be hindering you presently?

When do you most often experience God's power, joy and fruit as you serve Him?

Revisit our earlier question about "doors"...what doors of service might be open to you? What doors would you like to check out further?

"That Makes Sense...I Didn't Realize It Was That Simple"

"Here...use my iPad."

My neighbor Rob and I were sitting at a Starbucks having a conversation I had been praying we'd have for over a year. I'd given him a copy of my book, *The Day That Changed Forever,* which tells the stories of people who saw Jesus in His days before He went to the Cross.

"That was a great book...I loved the stories!" he said. "It answered a lot of questions I had."

"Thanks!" I said. "I'd like to hear more about what you thought." We agreed to have coffee and talk more.

Over coffee I asked Rob about his spiritual experience. Willingly he told me a story that's common to many... growing up in a church that talked about God but seemed more interested in money. As he became a young adult he drifted spiritually away from church and any connection with God.

When his two little boys went to a Christian daycare, he figured it was a good thing. When they got involved in a Christmas program at the church that sponsored the day care, he went to see it reluctantly. However, the pastor's short message at the end of the program touched him in an unexpected way. They started going to church again.

When I asked Rob where he felt he was in his relationship with Jesus, he wasn't quite sure how to answer. "Could I explain a simple way how to know for sure you have a relationship with Jesus?" I asked. He was eager to hear more.

As I've done hundreds of times before, I began drawing the simple plan of salvation known as the bridge illustration on a napkin.

"Wait," Rob said. "I want to keep this...here, use my iPad." I drew the picture and shared the Scriptures to show how sin separated us from God and how Jesus came to be the bridge so we could come back into a relationship with God again. When we put our faith in Jesus, the Cross is the bridge to God.

"That makes sense," Rob said. "I didn't realize it was that simple."

That night Rob clarified his relationship with Jesus. I went home with joy knowing my neighbor was now my brother in the family of God. He's growing wonderfully in his spiritual life and now is involved in ministry at his church...and leading his family spiritually!

God can use us in supernatural and eternal ways! Whether we use a napkin or an iPad, it's vital to be able to share the Good News of salvation in a simple clear way. That way anyone, anywhere, anytime can come to Christ... and someone's eternal destiny can change!

-Tim Roehl

8

Look Ahead

Prepare to Finish Well

Cheering Me Home

I was headed out for a run...a regular part of my weekly rhythm. Our beautiful four-year-old daughter Aubrey saw me in my running gear and followed me down the front steps of our home.

"Can I run with you, Daddy?" she asked. Her little freckled face looked up in expectation.

"Oh, Babyface," I replied. "I'd love to have you run with me. But it's too far for you. If you want to wait for me, I'll be back soon."

A bit disappointed, she said, "OK," and sat on the top step.

My loop is a couple miles and I'm not a fast runner, so I thought she'd give up and go back in the house while I was out running. Yet, as I began the uphill slope toward our home, I saw a little redheaded girl stand up as she saw me. She'd waited all that time for me to come home! Suddenly she began to cheer..."Yay, Daddy! Yay, Daddy! Come on Daddy!" She jumped and cheered for me all the way, her little face bright with joy.

I didn't run those last 100 yards home ...I floated on air. She ran into my arms as I got back and didn't even mind my big sweaty Daddy hug and kiss.

That's become one of my most precious memories.

> That's also how I'd like to finish my life's race...crossing the finish line to the cheers of those I love most... and hearing my Heavenly Father say, "Welcome home, son. Come share My joy."

What could finishing well look like?

How do you want to finish your race?

In the course of my journey, occasionally there have been signature moments that dramatically influenced me. One of those moments came when I listened to an interview with Dr. Robert Clinton called, *"Seven Habits of Highly Effective Spiritual Leaders."* He is a professor at Fuller Theological Seminary. His book, *The Making of a Leader,* has been similarly important to me.

In that interview, Clinton introduced me to the phrase "finishing well." It gave me a way to describe a longing in my long view of life. I want to finish well!

Clinton first gave the sobering statistic that only one out of four biblical and historical leaders finished well. That reality by itself makes me want to pray and depend even more humbly on the Lord and to ground my identity in Jesus. As Acts 17:28 says, *'For in Him we live and move and have our being...'* (NIV)

Clinton says we need to learn from those who have finished well. He gives Daniel in the Old Testament and Paul in the New Testament as examples of "finishing well." He describes "finishing well" in three ways...

1. They still have sweet, loving communion with God at the end of their life.
2. They are life-learners...they are still growing and learning personally.
3. They leave behind a legacy. They know their life has counted for something...that they have made "ultimate contributions" with their life. As Christians, they want to make ultimate contributions for God's Kingdom.

From his study of thousands of leaders from the Bible and through-out history, Clinton then highlights seven habits—internalized principles and consistent patterns—of people who finish well. Here they are in brief:

#1. *"A life-long learning posture"*

Too many leaders reach a place where they plateau and begin to stagnate or coast. A life-long learning posture is the antidote for that. Like Daniel, nurture an inquisitive spirit, read widely and well (or learn in the way that best suits you), learn from the lives of others, have an intentional plan for personal growth and most important of all, be a man or woman of God's Word! Let the timeless and timely truth of Scripture saturate your heart, mind and decisions. John Wesley, a man who read and wrote widely, described himself as "a man of one Book."

Clinton says this first habit is vital because knowledge is power and when we use knowledge well we have more ability to influence others.

#2. *"Effective leaders value spiritual authority as a primary power base."*

When I train coaches, I help them identify what gives them the credibility to be able to come alongside and coach others and empower. Here's a quick description of the four areas:
- Position--because you have a title or positional authority, people will give you a certain amount of credibility. However, if you don't use your position to add value, honor and empower people, you won't have ongoing influence. If you try to influence others and they feel forced, manipulated or coerced to do what you want because you have positional power over them, it's not healthy.
- Expertise—because you have knowledge and skill in a particular area, people will seek you out to help them. You'll want to use your expertise to help them be empowered themselves and not become overly dependent on you.

- Relationship—because you have a good relationship with someone—they trust you and know that you want the best for you, you'll have the credibility to walk along with them. Sometimes a friendship can make it hard for others to take you seriously, so your relationship has to have a deeper level of influence.
- Spiritual authority—people trust you because they see you lead and minister out of a deep, radiant relationship with God. They see God's wisdom and favor on your life and want to follow you because of that.

What Bobby Clinton calls spiritual authority flows out of a deep, humble, wise, pure heart overflowing with holy love. That's why it's so important to know the joyful reality of a Spirit-filled, Spirit-led life.

Spiritual authority also flows from leaders who have been shaped and formed by walking with God through suffering and what has been called "the dark night of the soul." They have been humbled by heartache, willing to accept God's discipline and stayed teachable. They are people of deep soul and wide influence. People respect and honor that kind of leader.

Clinton highlights the importance of spiritual authority to influence others because "people who don't finish well often abuse power."

#3. *"Effective leaders recognize leadership selection as vital."*

Clinton states that most organizations have a big leadership gap....they don't have enough leaders, they don't have a wise process to identify and equip leaders and they don't have a pathway for healthy leadership succession. Leaders who finish well know how to honor, encourage, equip, empower and release leaders who will do the same with other leaders.

When it comes to who winds up staying with a group long term, three principles come to mind:

"Culture eats strategy for lunch." Culture—"the way we do things around here"—can undermine nicely crafted job descriptions and strategy plans. Healthy leaders don't stay in unhealthy culture.

"No matter what an organization says on paper, it will always structure itself, choose its leaders and allocate its resources according to what they *truly* value."

"You choose who you lose." (or the tongue-in-cheek version, "You can't fly with the eagles if you stay on the ground with turkeys.")

#4. *"Effective leaders who are productive over a lifetime have a dynamic ministry philosophy (which means it changes and grows over time)."*

Clinton shares that our philosophy of life and ministry should be shaped by the constant fresh insights of God's Word, understanding our gifts, skills and personality and what the situation needs from us.

In other words, if you want to finish well, know how you fit and flourish and allow the Holy Spirit to lead you day by day.

I've made it a point to capture "life principles" that influence and shape me. What are some of your life principles?

#5. *"A sense of destiny."*

Wow. A sense of destiny is a huge issue for me. Clinton says, "A sense of destiny is:
- Realizing that God has His hand on your life, no matter what the situation may be.
- Experiences with God where He's revealed Himself and His heart for you.
- Knowing God has a special purpose for you that's bigger than yourself.
- Ongoing reassurance that He is with you and will give you what you need to accomplish His destiny for you and for His glory.

We all need to know that our lives matter. It's even more powerful when we have the supernatural sense of the Lord's anointing, favor, love and blessing. Our sense of destiny keeps us in the game when the going is tough. Destiny carries us onward and upward!

#6. *"A lifetime perspective."*

Here's a summary of Clinton's great insights:
- We need to have perspective about where we are now in context of the whole scope of life. Get the "lay of the land" to help you know where you are as you move from point to point on your life journey. The difference between leaders and followers is perspective. The difference between leaders and effective leaders is better perspective.
- There are three major issues on how God develops leaders:
  - The Process—God's always at work as He shapes us.
  - "Time" and Timing—things take time. God does certain things at strategic times as He shapes us. Looking at where we've come from helps us get better perspective on where He might be leading.
  - Our Responsiveness—when we cooperate with God, He will shape us to fit and flourish and have eternal influence. If we resist, growth and influence are stunted and stopped.

#7. *"Effective leaders perceive the importance of relational empowerment in their own and other followers' lives."*

We need mentors who pour into our lives out of their wisdom and experience, models and heroes who encourage us by their example, sponsors who speak well of us before others, divine appointments that God sets up and coaches who draw out what God is doing in our lives to help us discern reality, develop options and decide on action steps to keep us be transformed to be like Christ and join Him on His redemptive mission in our world.

Clinton notes that leaders who finish well had between 10 and 50 influential people invest in them over their lifetime.

In the end, everything flows out of relationships...our relationship with the Lord and the people He's placed in our life.

Coach Yourself Forward

What does finishing well look like for you? Write it down and describe it to some key people in your life. Listen to their feedback and encouragement. Lay it before the Lord and listen. He's with you and for you!

As we reviewed Bobby Clinton's key insights about leaders who finish well, what was most important to you? Why? What actions might you take to be more intentional?

Who are the influential people in your life? Take time to thank God for them...and thank them personally.

Who are you influencing? What have you learned about how to have a better investment in them?

What do you want on your tombstone?

"A good character is the best tombstone. Those who loved
you, and were helped by you, will remember you
when the forget-me-not flowers have withered.
Carve your name on hearts, not marble."
Charles Spurgeon

"Tim walked with God...
Loved his family...
Led others to God's best."
(What Tim wants on his tombstone)

"Have fun,
Do your best,
Let Jesus shine through you!"
(Roehl Family Motto)

Think about how you want to be remembered when you're gone. Not easy, is it?

Yet...when you reduce what matters most to a sentence—a life statement, what you want on your tombstone--it becomes your guiding principle for everything now and a homing beacon calling you all the way to the end of your life journey.

How do you capture what you want on your tombstone?

That depends on you. Some people ponder, pray, reflect, write and revise what they want on their tombstones over time until they come up with something that "clicks and sticks". Others have something rise up out of their heart spontaneously. Still others appreciate the help of someone who listens to them and then helps them capture concisely what they've heard.

The above statements came to me in two different ways...

My "tombstone statement" came as a result of a lot of prayer, pondering and revising over a period of time until it finally clicked for me. I would not have probably done it if someone had not encouraged me to think that far ahead.

I'm encouraging you to think that far ahead.

Our "Roehl Family Motto" came spontaneously as our girls ran out to the school bus one snowy Minnesota morning when they were young. I spontaneously called out after them, "Have fun...do your best...let Jesus shine through you!" Instantly, it stuck. It's been our family motto ever since. Though our daughters are now grown, we still say it to each other.

What has risen spontaneously out of your heart?

Since I'm a words guy and a coach, I've often listened to people and then given them feedback on what I heard them say, trying to say it concisely and clearly. Often I see a look of recognition as people nod and say, "That's what I was trying to say!" It's an honor to help people find their voice and validate their purpose.

Who is helping you find your voice?

Coach Yourself Forward

As best as you can describe right now, what do you want on your tombstone?

Plan a time where you can ponder and pray about your life statement. Put it on the calendar. Ask others to pray for you about it. Let it become part of process that continues until it "clicks and sticks." Others will recognize and affirm it with you.

What comes spontaneously from your heart as you think about what matters most to you?

Who helps you find your voice? Ask them to listen to your heart and give you feedback. Thank them for it.

What legacy do you want to leave?

Finishing Well

Surrounded by the forest, I walk not noticing the trees...
   until one catches my attention.

He is old.
 He is covered with worn bark and gray-green fuzzy
   moss.
    He does not project the beauty or power of his
      young contemporaries.

Yet...
 Yet there is a quality to this old, seasoned veteran of
   the woods that makes me notice and respect him
   more than the others.

This senior citizen put his roots down deep early, drawing
   life from resources I can't see.
    He has grown tall because he first grew deep,
      and stands above his younger, more handsome
        forest partners.

And...
 In spite of the fact that he has many more scars and
   wrinkles on the outside
    and age rings on the inside,
      he still flows with sap and fills his branches with
        leaves green with vibrant life.

This old warrior is finishing well.
 He has survived drought and storm,
   disease and pests...
    and still glorifies his Creator with the evidence of
      his life and influence.

Influence?

Then it hits me.

There would not be so many young, strong up-and-coming
   trees surrounding the old one if he had not gone
     deep,
       grown tall,
         stayed strong...
           and finished well.

They are not his competition....
   they are his legacy.

Written to honor Dr. Leighton Ford.... "Leighton, thank
you for modeling for me one who is finishing well.
You've allowed me to come under your shade and put
my roots down near you for this vital season of my
life." (Tim Roehl)

*At one point in my life I had the privilege of being part of
the Arrow Leadership Program, founded by Dr. Leighton
Ford. Leighton is Billy Graham's brother in law, and
served as part of Billy's team for many years. Many
consider him the greatest thinking evangelist of the last
half of the 20th century. Later in life, Leighton felt the
Lord calling him to invest in younger leaders. He felt his
greatest legacy would be through pouring into and
equipping leaders to "be led more by Jesus, lead more
like Jesus and lead more to Jesus." My Arrow experience
set the stage for what the Lord had ahead for me, and
I'm eternally grateful for the heart shaping and skill
equipping I received. One day at the end of my Arrow
experience, I was walking with Leighton. I tried to
express my gratitude for all Arrow meant to me and
how much I valued his personal mentoring. Finally I said,
"I don't know how to adequately say 'thank you'...but I'll
try to say thank you with my life."*

> Leighton turned to me, smiled warmly, and with his
> signature twinkle in his eyes, said, "We're counting on it."

The Bible has some powerful things to say about legacy. What we choose now influences our family for generations to come! Imagine the rippling effect of your life over the next 100 years or more.

God speaks about this in many places in His Word, but perhaps most powerfully and clearly as part of the Ten Commandments:

> "And God spoke all these words:
> "I am the LORD your God, who brought you out of Egypt, out of the land of slavery.
> "You shall have no other gods before me.
> You shall not make for yourself an image in the form of any-thing in heaven above or on the earth beneath or in the waters below. You shall not bow down to them or worship them; for I, the LORD your God, am a jealous God, <u>punishing the children for the sin of the parents to the third and fourth generation of those who hate me, but showing love to a thousand generations of those who love me and keep my commandments.</u>" (Exodus 20:1-6, NIV, my underlining)

My good friend Dr. Jim Smith gave me another important way to look at the verse that sheds new light on the way the Lord looks at the sins of the parents. Another way to translate "punish" is "to take an interest in a person...to inquire about someone; to be interested in someone; to take care of someone." A good shepherd is expected to take care of the flock; similarly he is expected to look for the lost sheep, to heal the maimed and to nourish the healthy. Jim believes, and I agree with him, that sin has generational consequences, especially in cultures where several generations live together. Yet, the Lord is always concerned about looking after and seeking to heal those who have been hurt by others. Our Savior, the Good Shepherd, is always seeking to redeem, reclaim and restore!

Our choices today have consequences that can last a hundred years or thousands of years! Legacy comes from living daily with a long view...with eternity in mind. It may be hard to boil a long view down into immediate and practical applications. Yet, an axiom I've heard over time has really helped me do both.

"Sow thoughts, reap attitudes.
  Sow attitudes, reap actions.
    Sow actions, reap habits.
      Sow habits, reap your destiny."

Ultimately, our legacy is in God's hands. Still, we can "live with legacy in mind." Here are some ideas to help you do that...

Start with questions like these:

"If the Lord told you that you could not fail and money was no object, what is your dream? Where would you be? What would you be doing? Who are you doing it with? Who are you influencing? How is God glorified?"

"When your family tells stories about you one or two generations from now, what would you like them to say?"

"What words or phrases would you like people to use when they describe you?"

Now...what can you do today and every day that will move you toward making God's dream for you become reality?

Pick one thing...go to work on it humbly dependent on the Holy Spirit's power with tenacious perseverance. Even when you don't succeed, get back up! God's with you! Get a coach to walk along with you and help you choose your action steps to keep moving forward. Live by promises like these...

"The Lord makes firm the steps of the one who delights in Him; though he may stumble, he will not fall, for the Lord upholds him with his hand." (Psalm 37:23-24)

"...for though the righteous fall seven times, they rise again..." (Proverbs 24:16)

Some of you are saying..."Hold it!" Trying to do that "dream/vision" thing drives me crazy. I'm just not made that way."

Good point...in fact, many people feel the same way. Bobb Biehl wrote a wonderful book called, *Stop Setting Goals If You Would Rather Solve Problems.* His intriguing premise is that many people are better at solving problems than they are at describing a dream. If that resonates with you, think about a burden you feel right now, a problem you want to solve, a difference you want to make on behalf of others. What does the situation look like?

Now...look out into the future. If you succeed in solving that problem, what picture do you see? That might well be a way to write a label of your legacy.

Coach Yourself Forward

What stories can you tell about family members who have gone before you?

What parts of their legacy do you want to carry forward into yours?

If you haven't written down your dream yet, do it now.

It you want to be remembered for problems that you helped solve, what would that look like?

When you consider what's coming in the hereafter, what is the Lord saying to you about what He wants you to know and do here and now?

Imagine eternity: our ultimate fit and flourish!

Our Bible College singing group was sitting in our hosts'
living room after ministering in church that morning, still
pleasantly full from our lunch. Someone asked the
question, "What's the first thing you are going to ask the
Lord when you get to heaven?"

A thoughtful pause enveloped the room. Then one of
our team, who was engaged to be married, wondered if
there would be marriage in heaven. Several rolled their
eyes and grinned knowingly. Another said they would
ask the Lord why there was such suffering in the world.
More murmured their assent. Other questions were
raised, each of them coming from sincere hearts.

Finally one young man in our group said, "The first thing
I'm going to ask is...how many did I bring with me?"

That question left everyone nodding in agreement.

After all, when all is said and done, isn't helping people know Jesus
so they may serve Him in love on earth and spend eternity with
Him in heaven what matters most?

"Only one life, will soon be past...
Only what's done for Christ will last."

"It will be worth it all, when we see Jesus...
Life's trials will seem so small, when we see Christ..."

Envision this incredible scene with me...

"After this I saw a vast crowd, too great to count, from every
nation and tribe and people and language, standing in front
of the throne and before the Lamb. They were clothed in
white robes and held palm branches in their hands.

And they were shouting with a great roar, "Salvation comes from our God who sits on the throne and from the Lamb!"

And all the angels were standing around the throne and around the elders and the four living beings. And they fell before the throne with their faces to the ground and worshiped God. They sang,

"Amen! Blessing and glory and wisdom
  and thanksgiving and honor
    and power and strength belong to our God
      forever and ever! Amen."

Then one of the twenty-four elders asked me, "Who are these who are clothed in white? Where did they come from?"

And I said to him, "Sir, you are the one who knows."
Then he said to me, "These are the ones who died in the great tribulation. They have washed their robes in the blood of the Lamb and made them white. That is why they stand in front of God's throne and serve him day and night in his Temple. And He who sits on the throne will give them shelter.

They will never again be hungry or thirsty; they will never be scorched by the heat of the sun.

For the Lamb on the throne will be their Shepherd. He will lead them to springs of life-giving water. And God will wipe every tear from their eyes."
(Revelation 7:9-17)

That scene is beyond our human comprehension and imagination... yet it's supernatural reality in heaven! Somehow the Apostle John describes his heavenly vision...this is what it will be like when we get Home!

"Fit and flourish" always has a "forever factor" in it...all we do in the here and now is an investment in what we will experience in the Hereafter. Our ultimate fit and flourish Kingdom contribution will be in the stories of the people we influenced for eternity who are now sharing life in Heaven with us!

Heaven! Home! Oh, try to see it with me!

Men and women, boys and girls from every nation...
...every culture...
...every language...
....every color...
...every strata of human society...
...every generation in history...
...all gathered around the throne of the King of the Universe, loved and redeemed by Jesus Christ the Lamb of God...pouring out worship, adoration, praise and unending gratitude! Home!

Untold multitudes are now free from sin, Satan, sickness, sadness, scars...never to be separated from their Father and His children again!

Waves of endless joy, worship, light, love wash over us as we bask in Trinitarian delight!

This is where we were made to fit and flourish...forever.

Coach Yourself Forward

Read Ezekiel 47:1-9; John 14:1-6 and Revelation 19-22. What are the pictures of our ultimate future as children of our Heavenly Father that thrill your heart?

When you think about "Home," who are you yearning to be there with you? Pray for them now.

Take time to praise God for what He's done for you past, what He is doing in your present and what He's got waiting for your future. Make them into good long "praise lists" and make them part of your personal worship in the days, weeks, months and more!

My Fit and Flourish Summary

As I Look Up

I see God as my....

I understand His will and calling as...

My relationship with God right now is...

I best relate to and connect to the Lord by...

As I Look Back

The significant relationships have influenced me are...

Significant experiences that have influenced me are...

I would describe length of my "seasons" as...

I am currently in a _____ season...

God is redeeming my suffering by...

As I Look In

I see myself as...

My identity in Christ is...

My personality style is...

My spiritual gifts are....

Things holding me back right now are....

As I Look At

My motivation comes from…

My strongest ministry orientation is…

My best contribution to a team is…?

On a team I need….

The people speaking inspiration into my life are….

As I Look For

"Fruit" The fruit I have borne consistently is…

My best skills are…

"Promises" My life verse is….

Promises speaking to me now are….

I am claiming these specific promises….

"Arrow" God is stretching, shaping and sharpening me by….

"Doors" The doors of opportunity and invitation I see God opening are….

As I Look Out

"See" God is giving me His heart for the world by….

"Feel" The needs in our world that stir passion in me are…

"Pray" I am praying for the needs of others by….

I am exercising spiritual authority by…

"Serve" I am now serving the Lord and others currently by…

I can see Him preparing me for…

As I Look Ahead

For me, "finishing well" looks like…

I want my tombstone to say…

The legacy I want to leave for the generations to come is…

When I imagine eternity, what thrills me most is…

My Fit and Flourish Summary Statement

God has made me to fit and flourish by…

Seven Checks For Knowing God's Will
Acts 1:24-26; Romans 12:1-3, Other Scriptures

The most satisfying place to live is in the center of God's will! Most people want to live in God's will, but don't know how to discover it in their daily living. God's will is not a mystery to figure out, but a relationship to be enjoyed. Here are the keys to know and walk in God's will.

I. Considerations About The Will of God

> "For it is God who works in you both to will and to do of His good pleasure." (Phil. 2:13)

God's will--more than His **plan,** it is His **pleasure**!

Discovering God's will must be saturated with **prayer.**

The top **priority--**"If you knew it, would you do it?" Getting your heart completely ready to respond to God is "90% of knowing God's will."

II. Seven Checks To Discerning The Will of God

1.The **Word** Check. God's will never disagrees with God's Word! (Hebrews 4:12; Psalm 119:9-11, 105; II Timothy 3:16,17)

> "The word of God is alive and active, sharper than any double-edged sword. It cuts all the way through, to where soul and spirit meet, to where joints and marrow come together. It judges the desires and thoughts of the heart. (Hebrews 4:12)

> "How can a young person live a clean life? By carefully reading the map of your Word. I'm single minded in pursuit of you; don't let me miss the road signs you've posted. I've banked your promises in the vault of my heart so I won't sin myself bankrupt... By your words I can see where I'm going; they

throw a beam of light on my dark path." (Psalm 119:9-11, 105)

Every Scripture passage is inspired by God. All of them are useful for teaching, pointing out errors, correcting people, and training them for a life that has God's approval. They equip God's servants so that they are completely prepared to do good things. (II Timothy 3:16,17)

It has the **_power_** to guide us and guard our motives.

Is there a **_particular_** directive?

Is there a **_principle_** that applies?

Are you taking the Word in **_proper_** context?

2. The **Spirit** Check. (Romans 8:14-16; I Corinthians 14:33; John 14-16)

"God's Spirit beckons. There are things to do and places to go! This resurrection life you received from God is not a timid, grave-tending life. It's adventurously expectant, greeting God with a childlike, "What's next, Papa?" God's Spirit touches our spirits and confirms who we really are. We know who he is, and we know who we are: Father and children." (Romans 8:14-16, The Message)

"For God is not the author of confusion, but of peace, as in all churches of the saints." (I Corinthians 14:33, NIV)

The Spirit will always **_confirm_** the Word!

The Spirit assures us we are God's **_children_**.

The Spirit is the Author of peace, not of **_confusion_**.

The Spirit both **_convicts_** and **_comforts_** us with truth.

3. The **Door** Check. (Psalm 32:7-9)

> *"You are my hiding place from every storm of life; You even keep me from getting into trouble! You surround me with songs of victory. I will instruct you (says the Lord) and guide you along the best pathway for your life; I will advise you and watch your progress. Don't be like a senseless horse or mule that has to have a bit in its mouth to keep it in line!" (Psalm 32:7-9, LB)*

Is there a **_door_** open?

Are you being led in peace or **_driven_** under pressure?

4. The **Motive** Check. (I Corinthians 10:31-33; Colossians 3:16, 17)

> *When you eat or drink or do anything else, always do it to honor God. Don't cause problems for Jews or Greeks or anyone else who belongs to God's Church. I always try to please others instead of myself, in the hope that many of them will be saved." (I Corinthians 10:31-33, The Message)*

> *"Let the Word of Christ--The Message--have the run of the house. Give it plenty of room in your lives. Instruct and direct one another using good common sense. And sing, sing your hearts out to God! Let every detail in your lives--words, actions, whatever--be done in the name of the Master, Jesus, thanking God the Father every step of the way." (Colossians 3:16-17, The Message)*

For whose **_good_** do I want to do this?

Who will be **_glorified_** by this decision?

5. The **Counselor** Check. (Proverbs. 11:14, 15:21-24; Romans 15:13-15)

"Without good direction, people lose their way; the more wise counsel you follow, the better your chances...in many counselors there is safety." (Proverbs 11:14)

"Stupid people are happy with their foolishness, but the wise will do what is right. Get all the advice you can, and you will succeed; without it you will fail. What a joy it is to find just the right word for the right occasion! Wise people walk the road that leads upward to life, not the road that leads downward to death." (Proverbs 15:21-24)

Allow others to "**check**" your checks.

We are not ultimately dependent on people, but God does **confirm** His will through His wise counselors.

6. *The* **Need** *Check.* What need does this decision meet? (Matthew 6:24-34)

"Don't ever worry and say, 'What are we going to eat?' or 'What are we going to drink?' or 'What are we going to wear?' Everyone is concerned about these things, and your heavenly Father certainly knows you need all of them. But first, be concerned about his kingdom and what has his approval. Then all these things will be provided for you." (Matthew 6:31-33)

There are two types of needs—**personal** and Kingdom.

If we seek first to meet Kingdom needs, God **promises** to meet our personal needs.

7. *The* **Fruit** *Check.* What kind of fruit will this bear? (Galatians 5:22, 23; James 3:13-18, John 17)

"But the Spirit produces love, joy, peace, patience, kindness, goodness, faithfulness, humility, and self-control. There is no law against such things as these." (Galatians 5:22, 23, NIV)

"But the wisdom from above is first pure, then peaceable, gentle, ready to obey, full of mercy and good fruits, unwavering, without hypocrisy. And the fruit of righteousness is sown in peace by those who make peace." (James 3:17-18 NIV)

Seeds planted now WILL bear fruit later.

Will this bear the fruit of the **Spirit**?

Will this unify the Body of Christ, or **split** it?

I appeal to you therefore, brothers and sisters, by the mercies of God, to present your bodies as a living sacrifice, holy and acceptable to God, which is your spiritual worship. Do not be conformed to this world, but be transformed by the renewing of your minds, so that you may discern what is the will of God --what is good and pleasing and perfect. (Romans 12:1,2)

There is safety, security and satisfaction in the will of God!

Endnotes

Chapter 1

1http://www.businessinsider.com/what-do-you-do-when-you-hate-your-job-2010-10.

2Trebesh, Shelly G., Made to Flourish: Beyond Quick Fixes to a Thriving Organization Intervarsity Press, Downers Grove, IL 2015. Page 179.

3Trebesh, Shelly G., Made to Flourish: Beyond Quick Fixes to a Thriving Organization Intervarsity Press, Downers Grove, IL 2015. Pages 11-12.

4Trebesh, Shelly G., Made to Flourish: Beyond Quick Fixes to a Thriving Organization Intervarsity Press, Downers Grove, IL 2015. Page 13.

5www.epm.org/resources/2009/Mar/28/great-quotes-prayer/.

Chapter 3

6Roehl, Tim, "Seasons of My Spiritual Journey," (self-published poem, 1997).

7Clinton, Robert, in a teaching tape titled *"Seven Habits of Effective Church Leaders."*

8Walling, Terry, *Focusing Leaders*, 32.

9Willard, Dallas, "The Divine Conspiracy," 337-338.

10Walling, Terry, *Focusing Leaders*, (Saint Charles, IL: ChurchSmart Publishers, 2003), 45.

Chapter 5

11Ford, Leighton, Arrow Leadership Program lecture, January 1996.

12www.youtube.com/watch?v=q4880PJnO2E.

Chapter 7

13Barrett, David B., and Todd M. Johnson. 2001. World Christian.

[14]Trends AD 30 - AD 2200: Interpreting the annual Christian Mega-census. Associate ed. Christopher R. Guidry and Peter F. Crossing. Pasadena, CA: William Carey Library.

[15]Baxter, Mark R. 2007. The Coming Revolution: Because Status Quo Missions Won't Finish the Job. Mustang, OK: Tate Publishing.

[16]Chacko, Jossy. 2008. Madness. Croydon, Australia: Empart.

[17]Far East Broadcasting Company. FEBC 2010-2011 Gift Catalog.

Finley, Bob. 2005. Reformation in Foreign Missions. USA: Xulon Press.

[18]Global Media Outreach. About Us. www.globalmediaoutreach.com/about_us.html.

[19]Gospel for Asia. Reach Millions with your Radio Ministry. www.gfa.org/radio/radio-impact/.

[20]Johnstone, Patrick, and Jason Mandryk. 2005. Operation World. Tyrone, GA: Authentic Media.

[21]Joshua Project. www.joshuaproject.net/

[22]Libby, Lauren. 2010. President's Column. 2010 Annual Ministry Progress Report 31, no. 2, www.twr.org/resources/progress_report.html.

[23]The Traveling Team. State of the World. www.thetravelingteam.org/stateworld.

[24]Weber, Linda J., and Dotsey Welliver, ed. 2007. Mission Handbook 2007-2009: U.S. and Canadian Protestant Ministries Overseas. Wheaton, IL: Evangelism and Missions Information Service.

[25]Winter, Ralph D., and Bruce A. Koch. 2009. Finishing the Task: The Unreached Peoples Challenge. In Perspectives on the World Christian Movement: A Reader, ed. Ralph D. Winter and Steven C. Hawthorne, 531-46. Pasadena, CA: William Carey Library.

[26]Winter, Ralph D., Phil Bogosian, Larry Boggan, Frank Markow, and Wendell Hyde. The Amazing Countdown Facts. Pasadena,

CA: US Center for World Mission. www.uscwm.org/uploads/
pdf/adoptapeople/amazingcountdown.pdf.

[27]World Evangelization Research Center. An AD 2001 Reality Check.
www.gem-werc.org/gd/findings.htm.

[28]Yohannan, K.P. 2004. Come Let's Reach the World. Carrollton, TX:
GFA Books.

[29]Yohannan, K.P. 2004. Revolution in World Missions. Carrollton,
TX: GFA Books.

[30]www.home.snu.edu/~hculbert/apples.htm

[31]www.ehc.org/free-prayer-maps.